CULTURE SHOCK!

California

Mark Cramer

Graphic Arts Center Publishing Company
Portland, Oregon

In the same series

Australia	Indonesia	Philippines	London at Your Door
Bolivia	Ireland	Singapore	Rome at Your Door
Borneo	Israel	South Africa	
Britain	Italy	Spain	A Globe-Trotter's Guide
Burma	Japan	Sri Lanka	A Student's Guide
Canada	Korea	Sweden	A Traveller's Medical Guide
China	Laos	Switzerland	A Wife's Guide
Czech Republic	Malaysia	Syria	Living and Working Abroad
Denmark	Mauritius	Taiwan	Working Holidays Abroad
Egypt	Mexico	Thailand	
France	Morocco	Turkey	
Germany	Nepal	UAE	
Greece	Netherlands	USA	
Hong Kong	Norway	USA–The South	
India	Pakistan	Vietnam	

Illustrations by TRIGG
Photographs from Mark Cramer

© 1997 Times Editions Pte Ltd
Reprinted 1998

This book is published by special
arrangement with Times Editions Pte Ltd
Times Centre, 1 New Industrial Road, Singapore 536196
International Standard Book Number 1-55868-361-5
Graphic Arts Center Publishing Company
P.O. Box 10306 • Portland, Oregon 97296-0306 • (503) 226-2402

Printed in Singapore

To Vanessa
the unwitting partner in this enterprise

... and even the winos wear roller skates
—Ian Shoales

CONTENTS

PREFACE

I thank all the perceptive people who agreed to be interviewed. Special thanks to my wife Martha, for her rational analysis.

A meticulous effort has been made to ensure that all names, addresses, and phone numbers are accurate. Inevitably, businesses fold, phone numbers change, and even reputable information sources sometimes contain mistakes. I apologize in advance if the reader should phone a hotel and end up speaking to a porno store.

In the interest of readability, footnotes are excluded. Quotes not originating from written sources come from the comprehensive bibliography at the end of the book.

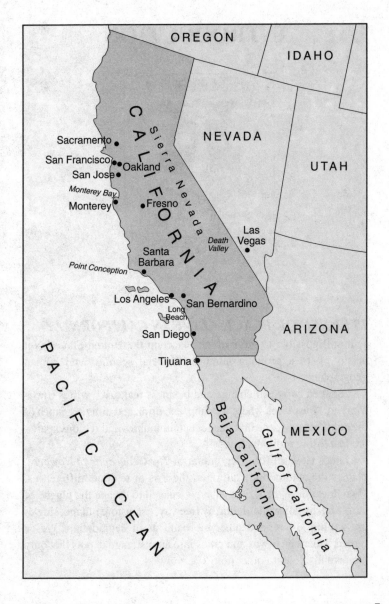

OREGON

IDAHO

C A L I F O R N I A

Sierra Nevada

NEVADA

UTAH

Sacramento

San Francisco
Oakland

San Jose

Monterey Bay

Monterey

Fresno

*Death
Valley*

Las
Vegas

Santa
Barbara

Point Conception

Los Angeles
San Bernardino

Long
Beach

ARIZONA

San Diego

Tijuana

PACIFIC OCEAN

Baja California

Gulf of California

MEXICO

INTRODUCTION

IS SENSE OF PLACE ALIVE IN CALIFORNIA?

Is it still possible to write about places in the United States? Not according to a growing number of social scholars and human geographers.

"Shaped by social change and business realities," writes Curtis Morgan, "the places where we shop, eat, drink and mingle – much of the cultural landscape that once set communities and regions apart – are fast losing individuality."

James Howard Kunstler, author of *The Geography of Nowhere*, blames the automobile culture on the loss of regional differences. "Few localities," he writes, "have managed to escape the plague of strip-mall banality, mutilation by freeway, chainstore pillage, single-use zoning idiocy, and other mechanisms of degradation. We've turned American towns and cities into auto storage depots that only incidentally contain other things."

In *Mapping American Culture*, Wayne Franklin asserts that: "It's getting hard to tell where you are in America. There is less and less local flavor."

Sociologist Ray Oldenburg, author of *The Great Good Place*, sees in this stagnating landscape a social and spiritual shallowness – a reflection of generations raised in sterile suburbia where prevailing values encourage "lifestyles predicated upon materialism and self-absorption."

"The fake is replacing the real everywhere," according to Margaret Crawford, chair of history and theory at Southern California's Institute of Architecture.

"The artificial environment is ubiquitous," she says sardonically, "because everyone knows the fake is better than the real.

"Theming," adds Crawford, "is the largest, most notable trend in architecture today." Orlando's Sea World creates a sanitized version of Key West. Universal Studios in Los Angeles imitates traditional walkable streets with its City Walk outdoor mall.

In his *A Walk Along Land's End*, award-winning author John McKinney calls this phenomenon "The Boutiquing of California's Coast."

"A unique coastal history is cheapened when the marketable is substituted for the memorable," writes McKinney. "Coastal architecture suffers when the frivolous is substituted for the functional. Coastal ecosystems are degraded when the expensive replaces the priceless.

In a personal interview, McKinney admitted that California is better positioned to retain its coastal splendor than other states. "Florida and Washington have nothing like the California Coastal Commission. The Florida coast is equivalent to the victim of an axe murderer."

McKinney calls himself a coastal activist.

"Theme parks – collections of shops and homes done in a nostalgic 19th-century style – complete the boutiquing," he moans.

"Three dominant themes prevail along the California coast: the New England seacost village, the Victorian, and the mission." Theming, he adds, is an "illusion of authenticity."

Modern trends against sense of place often emanate from Southern California. California invented suburban sprawl, freeways, and automobile determinism. Now it leads the world in drive-in restaurants and drive-by shootings.

"By subordinating so many aspects of our lives to the car," laments Kunstler, "we have created places unworthy of affection."

While prestigious critics lament the loss of sense of place, reproaching dominant trends in architecture, ecology, and town planning, on a grass roots level, a vanguard of California communities have been dedicated to preserving and cherishing what is regional and to nurturing on a more human scale.

ICONOCLASTS

As California icons stimulated modernist placelessness, much of the U.S.A. decided to march in step. Yet the greatest resistance came from within California itself, from a notable array of social heretics, whose views are now being taken seriously.

The assertion that California is the most different state in the union won't draw too many challenges from folks in other parts of the country, although regional variations are alive and well in places like Manhattan and the Mississippi Delta.

California has arguably produced more iconoclasts than all the other states combined. In the footsteps of Groucho Marx, a long line of irreverent satirists were molded in and nurtured by California, including Ian Shoales, Mort Sahl, Paul Krassner and Don Imus. Writers William Saroyan, Lawrence Ferlinghetti, Alice Walker and Charles Bukowski are but a few of California's literary rebels. From John Cage to Frank Zappa, California musicians delight in embracing musical and social taboos. The prevailing wisdom was that crazy people were hatched in California.

"At the end of the west is insanity," said professor Patrick Morrow, in reference to the literature of Ken Kesey, author of *One Flew Over the Cuckoo's Nest*. The great architect Frank Lloyd Wright added to the California mystique of craziness. "The continent is tilted," he said, "and everything loose rolls into California."

But critical thinkers have always been dismissed as crazies by spokesmen for mainstream culture. Lionel Rolfe, author of a book called *Literary L.A.*, is one of many social thinkers who debunk the craziness myth.

"Why," I asked Rolfe, "does California cultivate iconoclast thought as prolifically as it does oranges?"

"It comes out of the frontier thing. Restless souls migrated here."

In the conquest of the west, most pioneers found their ideal spots and stopped along the way. Only the ones who could not fit in elsewhere arrived in California, remaining there only because they had reached the end of the line. Ends of the line seem to attract nonconformists, as exemplified in other funky extremities of continental U.S.A. like Key West, Florida, and New Orleans, Louisiana.

The "end-of-the-line-for-restless-souls" theory is accompanied by other possible explanations for non-conformist California traditions. A second theory asserts that great icons breed committed iconoclasts.

Most great modern corporate icons of the United States are California inventions. If Barbie Dolls, Mickey Mouse and the celebrity industry had been born in Nebraska, that state, rather than California, would probably be teeming with iconoclasts.

Various California icons stood in the way of John McKinney's "walk along land's end" – a Marine base, a freeway off limits to pedestrians, a nuclear power plant, and condominiums by the sea.

"Would you still have become a rebel had those things not been in your way?" I asked.

"It was denial of access that made me a coastal activist," he confirmed. "People don't become rebels by theory."

Yet another theory is that California artists, writers and even business tycoons are often snubbed by the east coast intelligentsia, the heirs of Daniel Webster. The myths of California shallowness and the "Tinseltown" stereotype, were conjured up by condescending easterners.

Had California writers, artists and renegade business people been allowed into the exclusive cliques back east, they might have lost some of their motivation to create things that galled the establishment. (See William Saroyan's *The Daring Young Man on the Flying Trapeze* for an eloquent example of California's literary/social rebelliousness.)

Beyond these theories, California's richest natural resource is its unusual people. An offbeat element is often lured from other parts of the world to California in a process that might be equivalent to a "brain drain." The "renegade drain" siphoned in free-wheeling rebels like Upton Sinclair, Henry Miller, Aldous Huxley and Jack Kerouac.

Author Nigey Lennon believes that American writing all ends up here. In *The Sagebrush Bohemian: Mark Twain in California*, she asserts that Twain was formed in the west even though he didn't emphasize this period in his life. In California he had the space to develop his own strange self.

These influential nonconformist segments of California society are nurtured by multicultural townscapes where no one race or ethnic group is in the majority. Even California's ruling class has produced unruly daughters and sons. When Jerry Brown received the baton from his father and won the governorship, he decided to live in his own apartment rather than occupy the governor's mansion, thus saving the state money. He earned the nickname "Governor Moonbeam" for his weird ideas.

Today, from the pulpit of his *We the People* radio program, Brown has become a loveable misanthrope, calling himself a "recovering politician" and lashing out against "the corporate interests that rule this country."

California's iconoclast tradition has encouraged a state within a state. Against a foreground of placelessness and cultural homogenization are a profusion of truly different places, large and small, that have rejected the dominant fast-food-consumeristic landscape.

One seductively outrageous example of the nonconformist defense of sense of place is Critical Mass, the loosely knit organization of bicycle revolutionaries who use creative non-violence to defend the environment against automobile determinism. The term "critical mass" was used by urban cyclists in China who needed to gather in large numbers in order to safely cross busy intersections. In San Francisco, Critical Mass has been a monthly happening in which bicyclists clog city streets during rush hours.

The San Francisco hills and the earthquakes that formed them are one example of how the natural setting may stimulate nonconformism. The state's unpredictable landscapes are to geography what syncopation is to music. As we shall see in Chapter Two, the element of surprise and change in the geography has helped to conserve and enrich the state's sense of place.

California's human geography may be even more bizarre. The rainbow of diversity no longer fits the "subculture" label since California's minorities now form a majority. The Anglo-American pioneer migration from the east was balanced by Asian pioneers coming from the Pacific Rim. In some California neighborhoods, one may stroll between Korea, Philippines, Laos, Vietnam, Thailand, China and Japan within a few blocks.

The self-proclaimed Chicanos look like Mexicans and adopt United States customs but do not fit neatly within either national category. Within the most elusive folds of California is the mythical Chicano nation of Aztlán. Labor leader César Chávez, a pillar in Chicano history, ranks with Ghandi and Martin Luther King in the ethos of creative non-violent protest.

Blacks were involved in original settlements of California. In the civil rights arena, a reformer named Biddy Mason was the Rosa Parks of the 19th-century. (Rosa Parks was the first woman to defy segregation in the South and sit in the front of the bus.)

In the late sixties and early seventies, as the Black Panther Party was being hounded by the FBI, Panther leader Huey Newton once called for the assassination of Richard Nixon. The Panthers, with their breakfast-in-the-schools program, were mostly like peaceful cats, who used militant rhetoric to remind the neighborhood that they came from the family of the tiger. Newton's proclamation left him open to certain arrest ... until devoted surrealist and iconoclast Groucho Marx declared on network TV, with a snide grin, that he agreed that we should assassinate Nixon. Now, were they to arrest Huey, they would have to lock up Groucho too. The dynamic presence of minority groups in California has fertilized unconventional thought.

Notwithstanding the great trend toward uniformity in the United States, one can still write about a very distinct place called California, in great measure thanks to this state's rich history of unconventional thinkers and doers.

California's geological instability is but a metaphor for her contemporary cultural drama. Visitors will be entering an exciting story whose characters are in transition and whose plot is far from resolved.

Chapter One

SOCIAL SETTING

For centuries, no one seemed to want California. Technically, the Spanish colonial period began in 1542, when the expedition of Juan Rodriguez Cabrillo came upon California when in search of a "Northwest Passage." But for more than two centuries after the Cabrillo landing and the claim by Spain, an estimated 300,000 Native Americans in more than 100 tribes occupied most of California. An estimated one-half of the native population would later die from introduced deseases like smallpox and measles.

In 1579, Sir Francis Drake landed at what is today the prosperous Marin County. He too filed a claim to the territory, but the British, even less interested than the Spanish, ignored the claim.

In 1769, the Spanish got more serious about California, after rumors that the Russians lusted after the same land. A holy expedition with 300 soldiers led by Friar Junípero Serra set off to cross the region, over 1,500 miles. The Franciscan priest was 56 years old, a senior citizen by 18th-century standards.

Father Serra built the first mission at San Diego and managed to oversee the construction of eight more during the next 15 years. Of those Indians who had not died from exotic diseases, 60,000 converted to Catholicism, adopting Spanish surnames. The Spaniards rarely brought their own folk with them, and Native Americans accounted for 98 percent of California's population.

Father Serra is widely considered a hero of California history, while a few contrarian scholars claim the missions were "little more than Chumash concentration camps, and portray Father Junipero Serra as a kind of marketing expert, franchising missions like so many Subway sandwich shops."

In 1776, the year of U.S. independence, the city of San Francisco was founded. Los Angeles, founded in 1781 as El Pueblo de Nuestra Señora la Reina de Los Angeles, would remain a small desert town for many years in comparison with the growing San Francisco. Surprisingly, many of the original 44 settlers of Los Angeles were of African-American descent.

When Mexico Creoles gained independence from Spain, they continued to ignore California, but the region's Spanish colonists declared loyalty to Mexico. United States officialdom also harbored doubts about the worth of California.

"What can we ever hope to do with a western coast ... rockbound, cheerless, uninviting, and not a harbor in it?" said Daniel Webster in an 1832 speech to Congress. "What use have we for such a country? Mr. President, I will never vote one cent from the public treasury to place the Pacific coast one inch nearer to Boston than it now is."

Those words earn Webster marquee billing in "The History of Stupid Quotes by Brilliant People," consolation for all of us who have ever put our foot in our mouth.

In 1826, Mountain Man Jedediah Smith and his beaver trappers, the first white men to arrive in California, were condemned as spies and expelled from the territory.

Photo: Robert Holmes

The first Spanish Mission in California: San Diego de Alcala, 1769.

In 1841, wagon trains began carrying eastern pioneers to California. The territory was basically a patriarchal pigmentocracy. "The Indians are the principal laborers," reported John Marsh in 1836. "Without them, the business of the country could hardly be carried on."

By 1846, the future of both Mexicans and Indians was in jeopardy. "We find ourselves threatened by hordes of Yankee immigrants," declared Governor Pío Pico, "who have already begun to flock into our country and whose progress we cannot arrest."

Pío Pico would be the last Mexican governor of California. If he were alive today, he would be surprised to hear his exact words mouthed by California's current governors, who simply substitute illegal immigrants in place of Yankees.

Only the weather could hinder the advance of the "hordes of Yankees." In 1847, pioneers called the Donner Party were stranded by snowstorms while trying to cross the Sierra Nevada. Only 47 of the 87 trekkers survived, by eating the flesh of their dead companions.

17

President Polk's policy of Manifest Destiny triggered the 1848 Mexican-American War. Twenty-four settlers, who had seized Sonoma, California declaring independence in the "Bear Flag Revolt," joined the U.S. Army.

"Our armies are now in Mexico, and will soon conquer the whole country," lectured Naval Officer Revere to California Indian Chiefs. "But you have nothing to fear from us ... if you are faithful to your new rulers .... We come to prepare this magnificent region for the use of other men .... But in admitting others, we will not displace you, if you act properly .... You can easily learn, but you are indolent. I hope you will alter your habits, and be industrious and frugal, and give up all the low vices which you practice; but if you are lazy and dissipated, you must, before many years, become extinct."

Some slap in the face! Indians had done all the heavy labor for the Spaniards.

For years, California's indigenous population had co-existed, symbiotically, with the Spaniards and Mexicans. But with the United States well on its way to defeating Mexico, their days were now numbered.

On January 21, 1848, former slave and eloquent speaker Frederick Douglas wrote an article in Rochester's *North Star* criticizing a slaveholding president for prosecuting "the present disgraceful, cruel, and iniquitous war with our sister republic. Mexico seems a doomed victim to Anglo Saxon cupidity and love of dominion."

THE GOLD RUSH

Less than two weeks after the Mexican surrender to Major John C. Fremont in 1848, a nugget of gold was found at Sutter's sawmill. Had the Spaniards, whose lust for gold had catalyzed colonies throughout the Americas, found gold during their 300 years in California, they would have taken California seriously and sent hard-boiled armies to accompany the mellow Franciscans. California would have fought intensely against the invader from the east.

Sutter too had failed to capitalize on the gold. Sutter and his partner Marshall died broke after prospectors took over the land of the bankrupt Sutter sawmill.

Shortly thereafter in 1850, California was admitted to the Union as a "Free State," but the absence of slavery did not help the native populations. With the Gold Rush, white settlers formed posses to massacre the feared Indians.

The 49ers from the east were not the only wave of prospectors. From the Pacific came the Chinese. By 1870 there were 63,000 Chinese in the U.S., 77% of them in California.

From the gold fields of the Sierras sounded the Nativist cry "California for the Americans." A foreign miners tax was imposed, a "Catch 22" for the Chinese as a 1790 federal law prohibited them from becoming citizens.

According to historian Ronald Takaki, "California had collected five million dollars from the Chinese, a sum representing 25-50% of all state revenue."

In 1865, as the Central Pacific Railroad construction was initiated, a leit-motif in California history struck its first chord. White workers demanded that the company stop hiring Chinese laborers, who were depressing wages by diminishing the demand for labor.

19

Company superintendent Charles Crocker responded: "We can't get enough white labor to build this railroad, and build it we must, so we're forced to hire them. If you can't get along with them, we have only one alternative. We'll let you go and hire nobody but them."

Working through deadly snowslides with numerous casualties, the Chinese laborers organized a strike. Crocker cut off provisions and crushed the strike.

Descriptions of the Chinese by California entrepreneurs, eager to benefit from cheap labor, mirrored racist descriptions of blacks by landowners in the south. Racism was the universal tool to rationalize exploitation.

The Chinese survived the completion of the railroad, to become the primary builders of the California agriculture industry. The railroad served to channel produce to the east.

The Chinese were more fortunate than the Native Americans. The Modoc War of 1872 was to finish off the Indians as a significant sector of the population. Only 17,000 Native Americans remained, 3% of the California population. With the Gold Rush, San Francisco now had more than 150,000 residents. Los Angeles remained a sleeping giant, with less than 6,000.

By the turn of the century, just prior to the San Francisco earthquake, Los Angeles had already begun to catch up. San Francisco was nearing 350,000 residents while L.A. had surpassed the 100,000 mark.

The 1906 earthquake is now estimated to have been at 8.3 on the Richter scale. Although various tall buildings collapsed, the most significant damage was caused by raging fires from ruptured gas mains and blast furnaces. Nearly 500 city blocks were totally destroyed and 500 people died.

As San Francisco retrenched, Los Angeles reached milestone. At a ranch on the outskirts of L.A., later to become a neighborhood called Hollywood, George Van Guysling and Otis Grove began California's first film studio.

In 1916, the other major southern California industry got its start as the Martin, Douglas, Lockheed and Northrop families were granted government contracts to build airplanes for the U.S. Army. These engineers chose California for its cheap labor and low cost of living. (Today, even after the Cold War, the Pentagon keeps these companies in business with massive contracts, criticized by former California governor Jerry Brown as "welfare for the rich.")

In 1921, oil was discovered in Signal Hill (now Long Beach).

With film, defense and oil industries, the Los Angeles basin was destined to surpass the San Francisco Bay Area as a driving economic force.

But in 1918 the industrial yin was challenged by the environmental yang, in the form of the Save the Redwoods League, the first powerful environmentalist group. Efforts of this organization would lead to the first state parks. The clash between environmentalists and business interests was still firmly dominated by the industrialists, but California environmentalism would later steer the rest of the country.

GRAPES OF WRATH

With the Great Depression of 1929 comes the images of Wall Street, Morgan, Carnegie and the "old money" gang of the east. But it was the first elected president from California, Herbert Hoover, who ushered in the Depression. Conflicts between labor and California's "new money" were to catalyze some of the greatest literature of the thirties and beyond.

John Steinbeck's *The Grapes of Wrath* (1939) is the saga of the Oklahoma farmers ("Okies") who left their "dust bowl" drought in order to seek work in California's Central Valley, first confronting the type of border crossing problems now faced by illegal immigrants, and later, harsh living conditions and severe exploitation. (Today, visitors may walk the same Monterey streets featured in Steinbeck's *Cannery Row* (1945), although the original honky-tonk "joints" have been replaced by upscale eateries).

Never a revolutionary, Steinbeck was branded a subversive by agricultural magnates around Salinas, and was unwelcome in his own home town until later in his life.

The Central Valley also engendered the literature of Armenian-American William Saroyan. The Great Depression would influence the fertile prose of this great writer. Saroyan may be a precursor of contemporary iconoclast culture in California.

Saroyan was offered the Pulitzer Prize for his drama *The Time of Your Life* (1939) but declined the award to protest the commercialization of his art.

Both Saroyan and Steinbeck pushed the theme of colliding cultures to the forefront of literature. Culture shocks were as intrinsic to California's history as subterranean shocks were to its geography.

CONCENTRATION CAMPS

After Japanese planes bombed Pearl Harbor in 1941, one of the saddest episodes of the state's history would leave a stain on the whole nation. In February 1942, bending to Nativist sentiment, president Franklin D. Roosevelt signed Executive Order 9066, granting the Army "power, without warrants or indictments or hearings, to arrest every Japanese-American on the West Coast - 110,000 men, women, and children, most of them from California, to take them from their homes, transport them to camps far into the interior, and keep them under prison conditions."

Three-fourths of these victims were Nisei, children born in the U.S. of Japanese parents and therefore American citizens. The other fourth were *Issei*, born in Japan, who were prohibited from becoming citizens.

The Japanese remained interned for more than three years, with a 1944 Supreme Court decision upholding the forced evacuation on the grounds of military necessity.

The racial roots of the internment seem obvious when considering that white German-Americans, some of whom were active supporters of the Nazis, were not subjected to similar treatment. Racial motives were linked to larger economic objectives.

"We've been charged with wanting to get rid of the Japs for selfish reasons," stated an article by the Grower-Shipper Vegetable Association in the *Saturday Evening Post*. "We might as well be honest. We do. It's a question of whether the white man lives on the Pacific Coast or the brown man. They came into the valley to work, and they stayed to take over."

As Japanese internments proceeded, Nisei Richard Sakakida translated intercepted Japanese plans for the landing on Bataan, enabling the Americans to ambush the invaders.

The 442nd Regiment of Japanese-Americans was "probably the most decorated unit in United States military history," suffering 9,486 casualties, including 600 dead.

"General Charles Willoughby, chief of intelligence in the Pacific, estimated that Japanese-American military contributions shortened the war by two years," writes historian Ronald Takaki.

ZOOT SUIT RIOTS

In 1943, the Zoot Suit Riots were a prelude to later racial-cultural convulsions. Mexican-American youth wearing their typical baggy pants then called "zoot suits" were involved in an 11-day conflict with soldiers and sailors based in Los Angeles. Although there were no deaths, the racial taunting that precipitated the clashes would plant the early seeds of the Chicano movement. (Chicano refers to politically active Mexican-Americans with an underlying cultural nationalist ideology.)

A reminder of the Zoot Suit Riots emerges three decades later in Luis Valdez's drama *Zoot Suit*, originally performed by a United Farm Workers theatre group and later filmed in Hollywood.

As internal culture clashes escalated, the San Francisco Opera House was the scene in 1945 of the signing of the United Nations charter.

MCCARTHYISM

Richard Nixon, from Yorba Linda, California, was elected to the U.S. Congress after labeling his opponent, Helen Gahagan Douglas, "soft on communism." A primary target of the U.S. House Un-American Activities Committee (H.U.A.C.) anti-communist crusade was the Hollywood film community.

The Hollywood Ten, a group of ten screenwriters, refused to testify before H.U.A.C. and each was imprisoned on charges of contempt. (Martin Ritt's film *The Front*, starring Woody Allen, offers a powerful but humorous version of the period.)

Companies and schools fearful of H.U.A.C. asked their employees to sign loyalty oaths. At the University of California, 31 professors were fired for refusing to sign.

In 1952, Richard Nixon, a participant in the anti-communist crusade, was elected vice-president in the Eisenhower administration. Subsequent court rulings would find the loyalty oaths unconstitutional. David Saxon, one of the professors to be fired for refusing to take the oath would become president of the University of California in 1975. Richard Nixon will be remembered for the Watergate scandal that triggered his resignation from the presidency in 1973. The same Nixon who built a career on labeling opponents as soft on communism was to spearhead trade and culture pacts with his former communist enemies following his historic visits to the Soviet Union and China.

ICONS OF SUBURBIA

Suburban sprawl, nurtured by a vast freeway system, a virtual deification of the automobile, and a corresponding official contempt for public transportation, was a California invention that would spread across the U.S.A. Oil and automobile lobbies had persuaded officials to rip out the public train system of Southern California.

The whole notion of sense of place was threatened by the expansion of large chain stores and shopping malls, which siphoned away business from local downtowns.

Disneyland, in Anaheim, California ushered in a new generation of theme parks. Aside from Disney rides and cartoon characters, Disneyland "celebrated" precisely what was being phased out by the suburban mystique: Main Street U.S.A.

Suburban housing tracts were a type of sanitized substitution for more traditional neighborhoods, minus what sociologist Ray Oldenburg calls "third places" – public gathering places that offer an alternative to home and work (corner taverns, beauty parlors, general stores). Commerce was segregated into shopping strips in what was called single-use zoning. The social problems once addressed by the community itself were now handled by social engineers.

Garage doors were now built in front of the house, in contrast with the aesthetic conventions of the past. Parking lots for newer commercial establishments were placed in front rather than behind the buildings. One could now go from garage to store without stepping on a sidewalk. Front porches were replaced by back decks, further insulating the home owner from the riff-raff of street life. It was no longer possible to bump into neighbors without formally organizing block clubs. Foreigners visiting these neighborhoods were immediately astonished by the lack of people on the streets.

Those who bought into the suburban ideology sacrificed the spice of community in favor of a perceived safe environment that excluded the contradictions of the inner city and sometimes excluded non-white ethnic groups as well, in a real estate policy called "redlining." Redlining was later outlawed.

Southern California set the pattern for the trend of commuter communities, but suburban sprawl would later affect the human ecology of Northern California as well, as typified by Silicon Valley, a center for computer chip and technology industries, which extends from the south end of the Bay Area to San Jose.

These changes in the human landscape are symbolized by the move of baseball's historic Brooklyn Dodgers from New York to Chavez Ravine in L.A. in 1959. An old Brooklyn community was left without its quirky asymmetrical Ebbetts Field, where the enigmatic clown-bum Emmett Kelly was an icon. An old Mexican-American community in Chavez Ravine was torn down through Eminent Domain laws to make way for the symmetrical Dodger Stadium, not without considerable protest from that disenfranchised sector of the population.

One reached Ebbetts field via an excellent public transportation system. The hill in Elysian Park where Dodger Stadium now rests was scarred by an immense parking lot in an area reached most efficiently by automobile.

The old Dodgers were referred to lovingly as "The Bums." Old neighborhoods then reserved a place for their social misfits. But the new suburban ideology represented an escape from the misfits of society. Not surprisingly, the same Dodger players who arrived in L.A. for their first season in 1959 were no longer referred to as The Bums.

Meanwhile, more than a few California communities dug in against the suburban ideology in order to conserve more authentic places in the type of settings that the theme parks try to imitate, places we shall visit in Chapters Seven and Eight.

MORE ICONOCLASTS

The freeway culture was one of many California innovations to spread across the U.S.A.

"The apparent flattery the East Coast pays California," writes Richard Rodriguez, "is that the future begins here. Hula hoops, Proposition 13, college sit-ins, LSD, Malibu Buddhism, skateboards, beach boys, silicon chips. California, the laboratory. New York, the patent office."

Rodriguez suggests that geography plays a role in California's inventiveness. California's knowledge of the coastline makes her the elder and less innocent party in conversation with the east. "It is no coincidence," he theorizes, "that the most elegant literature cloudless Los Angeles has produced in this century is celebrated worldwide as noir."

The literature of California represents a countercurrent against the literary establishment on the Atlantic Coast. In the early 1900s, Upton Sinclair published his own books in California, "because New York publishers had proven fickle and unreliable. Sinclair was among a coterie of California authors for whom "journalism gave their writing a certain stamp that the New England Ivy League academics never had."

When colleague Sinclair Lewis accepted the Nobel Prize for literature in 1930, "he chastened the prize-givers for not having so honored Upton Sinclair."

Aldous Huxley was another great social critic to take up roots in California, spending much of his time in the high desert to the north of Los Angeles. Huxley's *Doors of Perception* was to influence those later writers of the sixties like Ken Kesey who were involved with mind-altering substances.

Writers who made California their adopted home and the home-grown variety like the literary anarchist William Saroyan were precursors of "The Beats" and other iconoclasts who offered a strange counterpoint to the conformist fifties. Jack Kerouac, Henry Miller and other counterculture heroes of their time moved to Northern California, which became the counterculture capital of America.

In the North Beach neighborhood of San Francisco, poet Lawrence Ferlinghetti's City Lights Bookstore served as a meeting place and performance site for the Beat writers of the time. Papa Bach's bookstore in Venice was the Southern California equivalent.

In the Bay Area, African American Jane Phillips was to write a blues novel called *Mojo Hand*, praised by Henry Miller but lost in the literary shuffle probably because it came from the "left coast." Phillips' book would have an influence on Alice Walker, another nonconformist California writer, whose *The Color Purple* would catalyze controversy two decades later.

"I read *Mojo Hand* shortly after it was published and liked it tremendously," wrote Walker. "Today, while putting the finishing

27

touches on my own novel, I picked it up again and found it just as real and humorous and solid as when I first read it."

In Los Angeles, the Beat writers of the fifties, lacking a San Francisco style community, were uncohesive and today are not associated with that movement. But writers like Charles Bukowski and John Fante may still be linked with that period.

This reporter did an unscientific survey in Paris in 1991, asking booksellers who were the most popular North American writers with their clients. Four authors topped the list, all of them westerners, and three of them Californians: Charles Bukowski and John Fante from Los Angeles and Richard Brautigan from San Francisco. All three Californians were devoted iconoclasts. The urban European sensibility seems more in tune with California nonconformism than with the eastern literary mores of the United States.

Photo: City Miner Books

Another iconoclast – Jane Phillips, author of the blues novel Mojo Hand.

Bukowski and Fante never fell in with the hippies of the sixties, but Brautigan was able to make that transition. Of the three, Fante's portrayal of California is the best example of the multicultural setting that would make Los Angeles the "Capital of the Third World."

These three writers made most of their money from European sales, and remained more widely read in California than in other parts of the United States. Brautigan's *Trout Fishing in America* sold two million copies throughout the world. All three writers stood by their small publishers at a time when corporate conglomerates were taking over the publishing industry.

UNITED FARM WORKERS

California was becoming the most populous and rebellious state in the nation. A cultural revolution emerged on many fronts. In 1962, César Chávez formed the United Farm Workers (UFW) labor union, in defense of migrant farm laborers.

The farmworker movement united culture with politics. Although not all farm laborers were Mexican Americans, they marched behind the banner of the Mexican Catholic Virgin of Guadalupe and sponsored musical and theatre events with rural Mexican roots. (In the early 80s, when the UFW was opposing mechanization of tomato production, this writer acted in farmworker skits playing the role of the exploitative landowner.)

The Chávez movement was essentially conservative and family-oriented. The radicals were the ones who were willing to create hard-skinned tomatoes with diminished taste that would withstand machine handling. But the state's growers, labeling the UFW as radical and subversive, enlisted support from police and the teamsters union to harass and beat the protesting farmworkers.

Chávez was to farm workers what Martin Luther King was to the blacks in the south. Both were schooled in the non-violent traditions of Ghandi and the followers of both leaders would be the target of violent repression. Eventually, the UFW spread to other states and

SOCIAL SETTING

became a cross-cultural movement. In a bold contrast to the troubled American organized labor scene, the UFW is in the midst of an aggressive comeback, under the leadership of Dolores Huerta. Chávez died in 1993, but the table grape boycott that originally expanded his movement to consumers has been reinstigated by the UFW because of the use of pesticides which endanger the health of both pickers and consumers. Through boycotts of grapes and lettuce, Chávez enabled consumers to identify with the workers who put food on their table.

Chávez's death came after two grueling days in court during a lawsuit in which one of the largest lettuce growers in California, Bruce Church Inc., sought damage awards for losses suffered from the union's strike and boycott. An appellate court ruled in favor of the union.

After 17 bitter years, farm workers finally signed a five year contract raising the wage of 450 lettuce workers to the minimum $6.62 an hour.

The United Farm Workers were part of a larger Chicano movement which would spread to other parts of the country with high concentrations of Mexican-Americans. (*Occupied America* by California State University professor Rodolfo Acuña remains the classic Chicano history.)

The Chicano movement is also responsible for the California street mural renaissance.

HIPPIES, BLACKS AND GAYS

If the Chávez movement was essentially conservative, the 1964 Free Speech Movement, beginning on the campus of the University of California at Berkeley, spread the seeds of a full-fledged cultural revolution. The hippies were officially born in 1967 across the bay from Berkeley in San Francisco's Haight-Ashbury district of Victorian homes.

More than 100,000 young people from all parts of the U.S.A. were drawn to San Francisco for the historic "Summer of Love," for peace, love and drugs. A typical California counter current of the time was the election of radically-conservative actor-politician Ronald Reagan as state governor.

The Vietnam War and the draft had much to do with young people opposing "the system" and "the establishment." Although blacks, along with Hispanics, accounted for proportionally far more Vietnam deaths than their numbers in the census, the immediate cause of the 1965 Watts uprising in African-American South Central Los Angeles was the charge of police brutality. Six days of rioting eclipsed the Zoot Suit Riots of the 40s leaving 34 dead and more than 1,000 injured.

Out of Watts was born the Black Panther Party in Oakland. "Black power" and black nationalism were seen as militant alternatives needed to complement the pacifist leadership of Dr. Martin Luther King Jr. The secret FBI crackdown against the Black Panthers rarely reaches mainstream histories.

Possibly as a means of deflecting black power influence, moderate Tom Bradley was elected as the first black mayor of Los Angeles, eight years after Watts.

The so-called "sixties" extended into the early seventies, as a gay rights movement, focused in San Francisco, became another facet of the cultural revolution. By 1977, gay-rights activist Harvey Milk became the first openly gay person to hold the office of city council member in San Francisco.

Milk and San Francisco Mayor George Moscone were assassinated a year later by the troubled conservative politician Dan White. White's attorney used the famous "Twinkie Defense," claiming that a sugar overload from that infamous pastry caused his client's brain circuits to trip.

When White was sentenced to only five years for the double murder, 50,000 San Franciscans clashed with police and took over City Hall in what became known as the "White Night Riot." It seemed as if each decade of California history in the second half of the 20th-century would be highlighted by a riot. San Francisco had proved that it had what it takes to compete with Los Angeles. But another great California upheavel was still to come, and Los Angeles would once more be the scene.

CONSERVATIVE BACKLASH

For many Californians. the cultural revolution had gotten out of hand. They had fled into suburbs but then found their idyllic dreams interrupted as social problems of the cities spilled outwards.

The election of Ronald Reagan to the governorship preceded other measures that would make California at once the most liberal and conservative state in the United States. A 1978 vote approved Proposition 13, a controversial amendment to the state constitution that limited property taxes.

With the cutback in tax revenues, local governments could no longer pay for the rising costs of city and county services, possibly an underlying cause of the 1992 L.A. riots.

What began with the election of Ronald Reagan as governor of California came full circle when Reagan was elected president of the United States in 1980. California had been the catalyst for an anarchist social liberation movement in the sixties and it was also the origin of the conservative backlash in the eighties. Meanwhile, as hippies became extinct in other parts of the country, this endangered subculture has remained intact in various regions of California, especially in the forests of the North Coast. No matter what one's political persuasion, it became apparent that the focal point for social change in the United States had shifted from the east to California.

Hoover, Nixon and Reagan, the three men who California has thus far sent to the White House, were all Republicans and were all besieged by major scandals during their administrations.

THE BIG ONE

People who willingly move to or live in this earthquake state are looked upon by others as eccentric for not fearing the "Big One," the expected major earthquake that would push the state into the sea. Thus far, these expectations have proven to be a false myth.

Yet the earthquake menace continues to discourage potential newcomers from less comfortable climates. California's stigma is its 1,200 kilometer scar, an earthquake fault called San Andreas. "California should experience a magnitude 7.0 or greater about seven times each century," writes the U.S. geological survey. San Andreas is but one of numerous earthquake faults crisscrossing the state.

Within the space of five years, it experienced two major quakes. In 1989, an earthquake centered only miles south of the San Francisco Bay area caused widespread damage with a few deaths, mainly motorists crushed when city freeways collapsed.

Few lives were lost as well in a 1994 quake in Los Angeles that caused shopping centers to collapse and paralyzed the freeway system. Had this quake occurred an hour later in full-fledged rush hour, the story would have been grimmer.

Traffic jams resulting from freeway collapses served as an incentive for Los Angeles to earnestly move on with the construction of a subway and mass transit system that would reduce the insane dependency on the private automobile.

In its initial stages, the slowly expanding system is working well, but many people are reluctant to use it, and fares remain steep as the public consciousness still conceives that freeway drivers deserve more subsidies than users of mass transit.

Experiments with electric cars are just getting under way. But as one Renault manager told this writer in France, "the electric car will simply transfer pollution from one place to another. You'll need more nuclear power to run those things, and you'll have to find a way to dispose of that waste."

Known for its poor air quality, the City of Los Angeles is not as bad as Athens, Greece, Santiago, Chile or Mexico City. At one time, employees of the Japanese Embassy in Mexico City were given vacations to Los Angeles as a respite from the polluted air.

THE L.A. RIOT

> *A riot is the language of the unheard.*
> —Martin Luther King, Jr.

In 1991, African-American motorist Rodney King was severely beaten by several Los Angeles police officers after a high speed car chase. In the consciousness of inner city residents, police beatings were nothing new, but this particular occasion was unique in that it was filmed by a video amateur.

When the police charged in the incident were later found not guilty by an all-white Simi Valley jury, South Central Los Angeles erupted once again. The verdict set off the social convulsion, but it was widely believed that poverty and hopelessness were the root causes.

"South Central Los Angeles is a Third World country," declared Krashaun Scott, a former member of the Los Angeles Crips gang. "What we got is inadequate housing and inferior education. I wish someone would tell me the difference between Guatemala and South Central."

Television viewers watched senseless beatings while police cars drove past without stopping. The public was apt to view the riots as "underclass" anarchy. A gang member known as Bone explained that the violence was "not a riot – it was a class struggle."

Historian Ronald Takaki saw economic underpinnings of the uprising. "Factories have been moving out of Central Los Angeles into the suburbs as well as across the border into Mexico and even overseas to countries like South Korea," he wrote. Conservative analysts trotted out their usual suspects, blaming the lack of jobs on illegal immigrants.

The attempt to blame one ethnic minority for the plight of another ignored the fact that both Latinos and African Americans were involved in the uprising.

Social critic Richard Rodriguez reflected that "the Rodney King riots were appropriately multiracial in this multicultural capital of America. We cannot settle for black and white conclusions when one of the most important conflicts the riots revealed was the tension between Koreans and African Americans."

The targeted Korean storekeepers had simply moved into a business void after white-owned commerce had left the neighborhoods. Those rioters who actually attacked Korean establishments failed to grasp a total picture in which large manufacturers, with zero Korean ownership, had given up on the inner city of Los Angeles and had withdrawn their businesses and the jobs they would have provided.

"The majority of the looters," added Rodriguez, "turned out to be Hispanic … here was a race riot that had no border, a race riot without nationality. And, for the first time, everyone in the city realized – if only in fear – that they were related to one another."

CIRCUS TRIAL

Fear of yet another riot may have indirectly led to the acquittal of O.J. Simpson, in the greatest circus trial of the century, the first one to be televised. Simpson, an African American football hero and television personality, was accused of murdering his estranged wife, Nicole Brown Simpson and her friend Ronald Goldman outside Mrs. Brown Simpson's apartment in West Los Angeles.

Mark Fuhrman, one of the policemen who had handled the blood evidence that would later be DNA tested, was a known racist who had made disparaging remarks against blacks. When DNA tests pointed to Simpson, many people, mostly black, were convinced that the evidence had been planted, while many others, mostly white, believed that Simpson was indeed guilty. In the wake of the trial, one more internal culture rift had surfaced.

The jury verdict and celebrations among blacks were "an emotional response to Mark Fuhrman, who stood for every white cop who ever planted evidence or was guilty of police brutality" commented African-American attorney Joan Wilbon.

"A lot of black people could care less about Simpson and see him truly for what he is, wrote Joan's brother Michael, a columnist for the

35

Washington Post. "They simply see this as payback, even if the score is still about a million to one."

Wilbon alluded to the power of the celebrity industry. "Simpson is free because he played football, because he turned that into a movie career and he's rich. Period. This doesn't symbolize anything or portend great changes in the judicial system to somehow ensure a better shake in the future for African-American citizens. Simpson is black, but it doesn't mean he spent any time *being* black in the larger more important cultural sense. It's funny we don't see or hear from these people in any social context until they're tied to the tracks with the train coming. Then, all of a sudden, they're black."

Ironically, Simpson's criminal attorney Johnny Cochran had represented Black Panther Geronimo Pratt a quarter of a century earlier. Pratt had been found guilty of murdering a Santa Monica woman. Cochran had successfully defended a celebrity who had shown no interest in black issues, but he had been unsuccessful in the case of Pratt, who had been politically committed to justice for blacks.

In 1996, Attorney Cochran discovered that the man who had testified against Pratt was an FBI informant (he had testified under oath that he was not an FBI informant). The accusation against Pratt occurred during a period when FBI director J. Edgar Hoover was conducting a crusade against black political movements under the code name of COINTELPRO. Phone files surpressed during the original trial but subsequently obtained under the Freedom of Information Act show that Pratt was more than 300 miles away in Oakland at the time of the murder.

Pratt's hearing for a retrial, with a more dramatic race issue, attracted considerably less attention than the Simpson spectacle.

The celebrity industry, so dominant in the U.S. economy, was the driving force in the ultimate Simpson show. A subsequent civil trial, brought to court by the families of the deceased and based on "probable cause" rather than "beyond a reasonable doubt" found Simpson responsible for the deaths and financially liable.

Virtually all major conflicts in contemporary California have cultural underpinnings. Issues that dominate current California history are illegal immigration, water wars, development versus the environment, and the future of the automobile. These themes will be examined in subsequent chapters.

UNSUNG HEROES

> *In France, philosophers are celebrities. In the United States, celebrities are philosophers.*

—Peter Carlson

Today the number one income producer in the U.S.A. is not automobiles, not heavy industry, not computer software. It is the celebrity industry. But history is not a series of biographies of famous people. Few took notice when the unassuming Mario Savio, who catalyzed the Free Speech Movement in Berkeley, died in 1996. Unsung individuals like Savio have been more instrumental in making an impact on the California cultural landscape.

California's environmentalism is a major historical current in today's world but few people know the names of environmentalists. Illegal immigrants desperately in search of sub-subsistence jobs are the cause of political reverberations from California to Washington D.C. but no one knows their names. Those who have rescued California towns and neighborhoods from strip-mall banality remain absent from history text books. The fact that lawns are green and agribusiness thrives in California's semi-desert regions has much to do with water conflicts whose protagonists remain anonymous.

Once visitors to California become aware of these great issues of conflicting world views, the celebrity scene will pale in comparison.

California is a stage for intrinsic culture contradictions. It is one of only three U.S. states that do not have a majority of residents of a single racial background, along with New Mexico and Texas. Everyone here is a minority. The largest groups of immigrants come from Mexico/Central America, the Pacific Rim, Europe and Asia. Recent immigration is only the tip of the iceberg. Visitors may be confused by this unwieldy quilt. Multiple cultural codes. Conflicting etiquettes.

As some Anglo-Americans fear losing their grip on California, they become obsessed with recent immigration and experience culture shock in their own land. Overt fear of Spanish and Asian languages has led to ballot measures that would repress the influence of Third World California. Other Anglo-Americans are thrilled to live in such a culturally eclectic setting.

So varied is California's cultural landscape that foreigners arriving from an exotic country in their typical dress will hardly draw a curious glance.

— *Chapter Two* —

PHYSICAL SETTING

An encyclopedic view of California would divide the state into ten distinct regions. At the northeast corner is the **Shasta Cascade**, snow-capped mountains, dense forests, limestone caves, fresh water trout, the bald eagle, rock climbing in a 225 million year old state park.

The northwest strip is called the **North Coast**. Jagged shorelines are met by rushing rivers that gash through otherwise impenetrable high bluffs. "Nature's oldest living skyscraper," the Coastal Redwood, has been around since the dinosaurs. Farther inland, rugged wine growing country.

The central east edge, called the **High Sierra**, bordering on Nevada, includes Yosemite and Sequoia National Parks. Names of nature writers and photographers like John Muir and Ansel Adams are engraved in this region. The giant sequoia tree is nature's largest living creation. Man made ski slopes at Lake Tahoe and Mammoth are impressive in their own right. Yosemite National Park is home to 2,400 foot waterfalls that polish shiny granite walls. California's highest peak, Mount McKinley, lifts its helmet-shaped crest over the region, at nearly 14,700 feet.

Just east of the High Sierra is **Gold Country**, with white water rafting, gold panning and mine tours. This is the home of Mark Twain's "jumping frongs of Calaveras County."

Still east of Gold Country and west of the coastal mountains is the fertile **Central Valley**, where the largest agribusinesses in the world extend in all directions beyond state capital Sacramento. The railroad museum in Sacramento may be the best in the world.

East of the Central Valley midway up the coast is the **San Francisco Bay Area**, including the cities of Oakland, Berkeley and San Francisco itself. Who hasn't heard of the Golden Gate Bridge, Alcatraz Prison, Cable Cars, Fisherman's Wharf, Chinatown, Haight-Ashbury (the original hippie neighborhood) and Lawrence Ferlinghetti's City Lights Bookstore?

South of the Bay Area, still on the coast, is the **Central Coast**, with John Steinbeck's legendary Cannery Row in Monterey, the boutique village of Carmel, the Pebble Beach golf course, Morro Bay, the Danish tourist town of Solvang, the William Randolph Hearst Castle, the artichoke capital of the world, and, Big Sur, the second highest region of rugged coastal bluffs after the North Coast, where literary luminaries like Jack Kerouac and Henry Miller found refuge.

Continuing south along the coast, we finally arrive in **Los Angeles County**, where the movie industry began at the turn of the century and hookers still linger on the raunchier blocks of Sunset Boulevard. The Santa Monica Mountains are the only mountain range in the world that separates two urbanized areas. L.A. still has its marvelous parks, including Topanga, Griffith and Elysian. This city is the home of Hill Street Blues, and the court building of the O.J. Simpson trial, the winding street where Laurel and Hardy chased a runaway piano, and scenes of famous criminals like the Hillside Strangler. The funky Venice Beach boardwalk has some of the best street entertainment in the world. At the opposite end of the county, the Los Angeles Crest Highway passes through snow country in the San Gabriel Mountains.

East-northeast of L.A. are the **California Deserts**, including the below-sea-level Death Valley, Joshua trees, the wildflowers of the Mojave Desert, the natural hot springs region made famous by Palm Springs, Zabriskie Point, and the gateway to the glitz capital of the world, Las Vegas, Nevada.

Crammed in an area between greater Los Angeles and the deserts is the **Inland Enpire**, with its Victorian homes and mountain skiing resorts of Big Bear and Arrowhead.

Along the coast, south of Los Angeles, lies **Orange County**, theme park country (Disneyland, Knott's Berry Farm). Past the coastal condominiums, hallowed surfing sactuaries.

Finally, south of Orange County, extending all the way to the Mexican border, is **San Diego County**, a semi-desert with green gardens, a world class zoo, a wild animal park, Sea World, and the La Jolla and Del Mar upscale condominium resorts.

IT'S OUR FAULT

Within these regions are earthquake faults, the largest of which is the dreaded San Andreas Fault, 1,200 kilometers long. Probable earthquake magnitudes along this fault are between 6.8 and 8.0 on the Richter Scale, and the average time between eartquakes is 140 to 210 days.

California's earthquakes, brushfires stimulated by the dry desert Santa Ana Winds, catastrophic mud slides (especially when the rains come in the wake of the brush fires), and floods from melting mountain snows should make it the disaster capital of the world. But California disasters are much more extravagant than dangerous, and many more deaths occur in east coast hurricanes, midwest tornados, and nothern ice storms and heat waves.

41

Photo: Siomara Cramer

House on stilts – could be dangerous in earthquake/landslide country, but many Californians believe they can dominate nature.

A CURRENT AFFAIR

The negatives of the disaster factor are eclipsed by the positives of California's eternal spring coastal region. Eighty percent of all Californians live within 30 miles of the coast and a benevolent Japan Current keeps the average high and low temperatures within a moderate range.

The average high in Santa Barbara, for example, 100 miles up the coast from Los Angeles, varies from 63° Fahrenheit in January to 77° in September. The average low in the same coastal city goes from 42° in January to 56° in September.

With the temperatures nearly always within the physical comfort level, rents in some preferred neighborhoods may soar above the financial comfort level, but exemptions from air conditioning and heating lead to lower utility bills.

As one moves inland, the ends of the temperature spectrum expand. The average high in Palm Springs in July is 108°. But the average low for the same resort city during its hottest month is a comfortable 73°, as the dry daytime heat dissipates as soon as the sun goes down.

San Franciscans complain about the cold, but the average low in San Francisco never dips below 45°, and the average high is always above 60° except for the month of January when it slips down to 55°.

For those who like diverse geography with year-round comfort, coastal California outranks the flat and humid coastal Florida. Although the ocean water is not as comfortably warm in California as in Florida, surfers don't seem to mind.

Californians who become weary of their moderate coastal temperatures are within driving distance of dry desert warmth, ski resort snow, or summer humidity in the Central Valley.

INSIDE CALIFORNIA'S GEOGRAPHY

The preceeding paragraphs recreate a Chamber of Commerce style outline of California geography. But something essential is missing from the official picture.

In brochures, California is out west, which is valid for the original Anglo-American settlers and the government that enacted their objectives. But for author Richard Rodriguez and other Californians of Mexican and Central American background, California is *El Norte*. The state's vast Asian populations traveled east to get here. The new diaspora of disgruntled Californians in Northern Arizona, Nevada, Montana, New Mexico and Colorado perceive that they have fled to the west, even though they moved east to get there.

Beyond the Chamber of Commerce photos of California beauty is an unsettled saga of the state's physical and human geography.

"Experience the lofty redwoods," says a brochure. But old growth redwood forests are the object of a major tug-of-war between environmentalists and the logging industry. In the northern forests, members of the environmentalist guerrilla group Earth First, chain themselves

43

to trees and suspend themselves 150 feet up in redwoods to prevent Pacific Lumber from cutting down old growth trees, while a group called EPIC, headed by a former Zen student, uses legal means to fight the same logging company.

The once environmentally conscious Pacific Lumber had intensely escalated its cutting only after a Texan by the name of Charles Hurwitz had acquired the company through his Maxxam Group Inc. The acquisition came about with the selling of junk bonds through the "legendary pope of junk bonds" Michael Milken (later convicted of securities fraud). Pacific Lumber was now obligated to cut down trees with a frenzy in order to meet its bond obligations. Braking the operation were environmentalist organzations whose members belong to the Mateel, capital of the hippie nation, a subculture named for the two major rivers that would be effected by erosion, the Mattole and the Eel.

An encyclopedia might remark that California's sea coast is lined by an attractively rugged chain of coastal mountains but ignores the conflicts that rise and ebb over the public's access to this unique coast. From Imperial Beach at the extreme south to Venice Beach in Los Angeles, residents have been battling developers to maintain public access to their beaches and prevent gentrification. John McKinney himself proudly proclaims that citizen activism has meant that "surprisingly, a more creative interface with the natural world is occurring in that metropolis of Los Angeles."

Chambers of Commerce might applaud the manicured lawns and kaleidoscopic gardens of Southern California, from San Diego to Santa Barbara, but water wars rage over distribution of this precious resource. Agribusiness uses more than eight of every ten gallons of California's water, receiving 6.8 billion in water subsidies; wetlands tourism and the fishing industry are adversely affected. Once rich watersheds 300 miles to the north have been depleted in order to maintain English lawns in semi-arid Southern California.

Yosemite is praised in tourist pamphlets as a spectacular haven of mountains, gorges, meadows, alpine lakes, waterfalls, and sculpted

Photo: Robert Holmes

Vernal Falls, Yosemite National Park.

rock, without mentioning that a new version of "Fatal Attraction" is threatening the future of the park. Four million visitors per year are lured by Yosemite's rugged beauty. Individually, most visitors respect the glorious Yosemite, but as a multitude, they endanger the park.

Tourist departments will laud California's Central Valley as the world's greatest bread basket and fruit bowl. But in order to run these gigantic farming operations, which in the distance off Route 5 resemble surreal Yves Tanguy cityscapes, migrant laborers live and work in subhuman conditions. Ever more powerful pesticides are used as mutating pests develop chemical resistence. Large scale

45

agriculture reduces crop diversity. Diminshed diversity heightens vulnerability to widespread epidemics.

As corporate agriculture becomes unwieldy beyond a certain threshold, alternative forms of micro-farming and organic agriculture are now on the rise, as typified by the Fetzer Vineyards in Hopland, California, with the state's first organically grown wines.

Even California's famous brush and forest fires have led to ideological conflict. See a fire, put it out; that's the conventional wisdom. But "fire is actually a beneficial pruning process," writes John McKinney.

Trespassing on the California Coast

The John McKinney story is an overture to the next chapter, a character sketch of California. Mckinney's daily life exemplifies how setting and character may merge.

One of the first acts of the California visitor is a Pacific Ocean baptism. But at a number of points along the coast, your access may be blocked by "human architecture at its worst – the cell-block style of Condominium Shores." John McKinney wrote those lines in his *A Walk Along Land's End*, a lyrical account of his attempt to forge a 1,700 mile walking trail along the seacoast from the Mexican border at the south to the northern border at Oregon.

To meet his objective, McKinney found it necessary to become a trespasser, over a bridge at San Diego that prohibited pedestrian traffic (confonting the icon he labels "Motoris Californicus"), through the off-limits territory of the San Onofre Nuclear Power Plant, across the forbidden edge of the Camp Pendleton Marine Base, and through various private properties of resorts and family compounds whose western limits reached right up to the edge of the Pacific Ocean.

"Maybe I'm getting too old to be a rebel. Maybe not," wrote this nature columnist and surfer as he contemplated embarking on another of his trespassing escapades. "Why should sixteen be the only society sanctioned age for rebellion. Like wine, rebellion tastes better with age."

For McKinney, beach front condominium developments proved a greater obstacle than the marine base or nuclear power plant. The seafront condominium is a California icon. McKinney's need to merge with California's coastal geography came into conflict with that icon. This is the story of how icons breed iconoclasts.

"The sight of the huge, charmless, condominium-surrounded Marina takes the wind out of my sails," he wrote, lamenting " ... a Seal beach without a seal, a Laguna Beach without a laguna."

But the geography itself fights back as some of these "castles in the sand" are expected to be defeated by the natural erosion process.

Much of the sea blocking "condomania" was found in Orange County, and why not? The Disneyland ideology promotes fantasy over reality. Farther north, McKinney had to confront what he calls "the boutiquing of California's coast," in Carmel and Monterey, to the south of San Francisco.

In his trespassing escapades, McKinney was met by the point of a gun, the growl of an enraged guard dog and the ticket pad of a California highway patrolman.

Fortunately, much of California's seacoast is still accessible, and people like McKinney are part of an ongoing struggle to save what is still free and to provide public access to those parts that have become someone's real estate. In essence, the diametrically opposed ideologies of public access versus private control represent an intrinsic California culture clash.

North of the Golden Gate recreation area on the Point Reyes Peninsula is for McKinney an exquisite example of coastal access.

"The coast trait here is a true world-class footpath," says McKinney. "It's Euro-walking with a California flavor."

Farther north on the North Coast, the geography has taken things into its own hands. The inconceivably rugged bluffs and the raging rivers splitting them have been largely successful in preventing housing developments. One of the few housing complexes to go up on this coast soon became a virtual ghost town after being condemned to solitary confinement by the surrounding bluffs.

47

McKinney's objective is the "adoption of the English footpath system – that is to say, hikers are allowed right of passage over private land in exchange for civilized behavior on all parts."

Various non-profit groups such as Coast Walk in Sonoma County and the California Coastal Trails Foundation are involved in an ongoing struggle against the real estate industry and government bureaucracy to liberate the coastline.

Attempts to tame the disobedient California terrain become the theme of many individual dramas. Canyon lovers build houses on stilts, in order to enjoy a spectacular view from high cliffs into the deep gorges, on either side of the fabled Mulholland Drive in Los Angeles, where geologists have labeled the subsoil unstable.

Status seekers wishing to become part of the Malibu elite are willing to build mansions in the middle of fire and landslide country just above the Pacific Coast Highway north of Los Angeles. They get free publicity for their next movie when a brush fire rages through their home.

California geography has been a major player in numerous conflicts, some of them violent. The conflicts are based on opposing cultural views regarding the relationship between human beings and geography: to dominate nature or to become a humble part of it.

California is condemned by its beauty and natural wealth to be the scene of contested struggles whose outcomes will influence how the rest of the world deals with major issues of land, water, forests and crosscultural populations.

California is one of the few dramas on the world stage where physical and human setting moves from the background to the foreground and becomes part of a spectacular plot.

— Chapter Three —

MEET SOME CALIFORNIANS

In this chapter we meet some of the unsung protagonists in the California story. We begin to explore a vital question: will California's extraordinary characters be able to overcome the intrinsic culture clashes of the region's history and mold a stable environment for a thriving multicultural society, or will "the big one," the ultimate culture quake, lead to greater polarization?

THE RETURN OF SALLY BELL

As the Civil War raged in the east, a frightened Native American child named Sally Bell hid herself in California's North Coast forests while U.S. soldiers massacred her family and tribe.

For thousands of years, the North Coast was one of the most populated areas of prehistoric North America, including the Pomo, Wailaki and Yuki peoples, who coexisted with the redwood and oak forests as fishers and gatherers, nourishing themselves on seeds, nuts, berries, roots, seaweed, salmon and perch, and curing themselves with natural medicines.

Thousands of native peoples were slaughtered on the North Coast during the decades following the Gold Rush, while other Indians scattered to safer refuge. After 14,000 years of balance between nature and human impact, the North Coast began a new period in which human beings were bent on dominating the region for economic gain.

One example of the transformation: the Sinkyone people sustained the oak forests by burning the underbrush and the worm-infested acorns, but the newcomers stripped the oaks of their bark, to be used for tanning leather, leaving the naked trees to rot. By the 1920s, a large part of the Sinkyone region had lost its living adult oak population.

From 1880 it took 100 years to log 98% of the Sinkyone's old growth redwoods. Most of the losses occurred after World War II through mechanized logging.

"Although timber companies like to speak of their business as agriculture," wrote William Poole for *Sierra Magazine*, "clearcutting an old-growth forest is more like mining gold than like growing corn: once harvested, the forest cannot return for many human lifespans." When the forest goes, other resources go with it. Erosion from industrial logging allows silt to clog salmon streams.

In 1911, British travel writer John Smeaton Smith called these forests the finest he'd ever seen. With all the devastation since then, both human and ecological, one would think that the California North Coast rainforest would have been reduced to a misty legend.

But geography itself worked to shield the forest. The more than 3,800 acres of seaside mountains are "so convoluted that California's main coastal highway never invaded them."

When in the 1970s, a bulletin board at the state park's Needle Rock visitors' center proclaimed the Sinkyone a "vanished people," local Indians objected. Native Americans organized to defend and expand the park. In 1983, allied environmentalists and Native Americans drew a border around the area they had decided to defend. They perched themselves in some trees and formed human chains around others that were slated to be cut by the Georgia-Pacific Corporation. When police arrived to arrest the demonstrators, one of them gave her name as Sally Bell.

In 1986, a coalition of the Environmental Information Center, the National Indian Treaty Council, and the Sierra Club, purchased 7,100 acres from the lumber company. The spectacular coastal strip and redwood groves like the one named for Sally Bell were added to the existing Sinkyone Wilderness State Park.

Lumber companies customarily threaten local residents with the job-loss argument when their cutting is challenged. But eco-tourism and the revitalization of salmon streams is expected to create new employment opportunities in the expanded park, which includes redwood, Douglas fir and oak forests, once-endangered wildlife like the spotted owl and the marbled murrelet, meadows, campsites, estuaries, and a half-crescent beach.

Native Americans will now run the park, a symbolic and historic victory. Hawk Rosales, an Apache silversmith, saddlemaker, and horse trainer is the executive director of the InterTribal Sinkyone Wilderness Council.

Old logging roads will be rehabilitated by planting native grasses and trees, and under the control of native peoples, limited logging will be permitted, with a statute guaranteeing a sustainable, mature forest.

According to the stipulation, the mature redwood-fir forest should look like a multi-story canopy, with a mix of native vegetation from different ages. Neither old-growth harvesting nor cutting near stream corridors, steep slopes or in the habitat of endangered birds will be permitted.

This marks a return to the Sally Bell era, when native peoples harvested resources without using them up. Before visiting the

Sinkyone InterTribal Park, send for information at 190 Ford Road, #333, Ukiah, California 95482 or phone (707) 463-6745.

A NIGHT IN GANGLAND

Outsiders think of Compton, a blue-collar suburb south of Los Angeles, as a gangland hub. With my car at the mechanic, I found myself on a dark corner of an eerie Compton neighborhood, waiting for a bus on my way to Los Angeles from California State University at Long Beach.

I'd lived in the gang-infested Pico-Union neighborhood just west of downtown. The nearest I'd come to witnessing a gang culture confrontation was bumping into several street-corner, glue sniffing teens. They were outfitted like the typical Mexican-American "cholo" subculture, with baggy pants whose waist bands rested below the hip without somehow falling down. Their shiny black hair began low on the forehead and was combed straight back.

"You're blowing your brains out with that glue," I said.

"Yeah, we know," one of them grinned, and went back to sniffing. Those kids would be recruited by the infamous 18th Street Gang, and maybe get to be passengers in a drive-by shooting.

Remember the aria-like hit pop tune "McArthur Park"? That park is one of the raunchy spots in Pico-Union. You see bars with Latin music, the smell of urine coming from the bathroom, stores with cheap goods flowing out onto the sidewalk, in-and-out motels for short sexual liaisons, with hourly charges, tenements with exposed electrical wires and wall-to-wall cockraoches inhabited by illegal immigrants and Salvadoran refugees.

I knew Pico-Union well enough to feel comfortable there. But Compton was strange territory for me. I was enveloped in a vague cloud of anxiety about waiting on a street corner at prime-time TV hours, when residents were glued to their sets. No one's eyes were on the streets.

A sixteen-year-old at the bus stop told me the kids at school would chide him about the pre-teen sound of his unchanged voice.

"They call me Bear," he said. "You can tell by the way I look."

"Who calls you Bear? Your folks? The kids in school?"

"The guys in the gang," he said.

In L.A. County after rush hour, buses make rare appearances. We had time to chat. There were no fast food joints around, no walk-in businesses open, nowhere to run in case of stray gunshots.

Modern commercial lighting systems had not yet arrived at the stucco facades of this particular small business street. On the side streets, lined with tall swaying palm trees were 1930's vintage homes, the ones that still had plaster and lath walls instead of drywall.

"So why'd you join the gang?" I asked.

Bear didn't answer. Instead, he lifted his sweatshirt, baring a chest whose breasts were protruding enough to make you wonder which side of the sex line he was on. At first I assumed that his breasts were part of the context of a chubby frame, maybe extra baggage from too many Big Macs. But Bear was telling me in his own way that he was not an ordinary human specimen.

He was telling me what I had learned from professor Ramón Salcido at U.S.C., that gangs became family for society's outcasts.

53

Salcido's example was a group of institutionalized deaf-mutes who became the best warriors for an East L.A. gang. The gang was the only societal establishment to accept them the way they were.

Folks from middle class suburbs look at gangs as a race issue. The L.A.P.D. recognizes 230 black and Latino gangs and some 80 Asian gangs. But first-generation Latin American, African and Asian immigrants who come here with a sense of national pride rarely participate in gangs. The ones who are born in the U.S.A. but do not fit in with the dominant culture seem more apt to join.

Bear's gang is Latino. He tells me how his friends engage in late-night guerrilla spray-paint attacks on nearby factories, then approach factory managers the next day for freelance jobs cleaning up the graffiti.

Nobel Prize winner Octavio Paz's essay on the "pachuco" from his *The Labyrinth of Solitude* still seems valid today, nearly a half century after its publication date, except the pachuco is now referred to as the "cholo." Paz believed that the social alienation of the cholo resulted from the fact that his Mexican-American heritage made him an outsider in U.S. society while, with his "Spanglish" accent and intonation, he was not accepted in Mexico either.

In France, a similar phenomenon exists with the "beurs," French born youth of North African Arabic descent who are marginalized from the dominant French society yet would not be accepted in places like Tunisia and Algeria.

Paz's essay predated the Chicano movement that attempts to provide the national identity so lacking in the cholos. Professor Salcido introduced me to several ex-gang members, now working to save youth from the gang culture, who proudly affirmed that they had discovered themselves through Chicano activism and an identity with the mythical nation of Aztlán. Aztlán is not listed in Rand McNally maps, but could be superimposed over the southwest of the U.S. and the north of Mexico.

Bear knows nothing of the Chicanos. His gang and its turf are his nation.

Beauty and the beasts. Rival gang members cross paths, or a drug deal gone bad? Beating in front of a Venice mural.

I once worked with a Latin American community organization in which Chicano members insisted on occupying the main decision-making positions because Mexican members who had attended school in Mexico already possessed the self-esteem that comes when you belong to an identifiable nation.

A Korean gang member shared his feelings about a similar cultural void. His father, a storekeeper, would work 14 hours a day, and was proud to put food on the table and pay for the needs of his family.

"But I would see American fathers in the parks and on TV hugging their kids," he said. "My father never hugged me. It's just not his way. He's a good man. But for me, the gang is family."

Two opposite but parallel trends may be observed in the California gang scene. On the one hand, the crack cocaine epidemic, which began in the early eighties, escalated the level of violence as guns increasingly replaced fists and knives. On the other hand, thanks to a wave of community policing measures and truces between warring gangs, Los Angeles and other California cities are a good deal safer than urban centers like Atlanta, Miami, Detroit, Chicago, and Washington, D.C., according to a survey conducted by *Money Magazine*.

Back in the 80s, gang violence intensified after a new, cheaper version of cocaine called crack was introduced to the African American neighborhoods of South Central Los Angeles. A controversial 1986 series in the *San José Mercury* by Gary Webb cited court testimony that a black gang member, Freeway Ricky Ross, had been supplied with dirt cheap crack cocaine from Danilo Blandon and Norwin Meneses, two Nicaraguans with alleged ties to the CIA who were raising money for the CIA-backed "Contra" war against the Sandinistas. African American leaders were incensed and began an organized protest.

"Whatever we were running," testified Blandon, "the profit was going for the Contra revolution."

"It is one of the most bizarre alliances," wrote Webb. "The union of a U.S. backed army attempting to overthrow a revolutionary socialist government and Uzi-toting 'gangstas' of Compton and South Central Los Angeles."

Two former Drug Enforcement Administration officers, Michael Levine and Celerino Castillo III have added their own accusations that the CIA was connected in some way with drug sales that supported the Contras.

At the same time, Gary Webb was accused by major newspapers of irresponsible journalism. But when Webb's editor wrote the *Post* with a response, the *Post* decided not to print it.

A *Post* "Ombudsman" column by Geneva Overholser, added to the criticism that the *San José Mercury* series was "flawed." But she criticized the dailies for bickering on the excesses of the Webb series while not recognizing its substance.

"In fact," continued Overholser, "as *Post* editors and reporters knew ... there was strong previous evidence that the CIA at least chose to overlook Contra involvement in the drug trade."

No major newspaper questioned the fact that Freeway Ricky Ross, the Contra contact, was responsible for selling crack in South Central Los Angeles, but *L.A. Times* reporter Jesse Katz minimized Webb's Contra-Ricky Ross connection by writing that Ross was one of many "interchangeable characters" who was "dwarfed" by other dealers. "How the crack epidemic reached that extreme, on some level, had nothing to do with Ross," Katz reported (October 20 1996).

The only problem was that prior to the Gary Webb articles that Katz was attempting to debunk, the same Katz had written: "…if there was a criminal mastermind behind crack's decade-long reign, if there was one outlaw capitalist most responsible for flooding Los Angeles' streets with mass-marketed cocaine, his name was Freeway Rick" (December 20 1994).

Conradictory reports like those of Katz prompted thousands of demonstrators in February of 1997 to accuse the *L.A. Times* of attempting to whitewash the story of official U.S. government complicity in the flow of crack into L.A.

At a Santa Monica forum attended by this author, Gary Webb said that the media giants were embarrassed by not having uncovered the story and were now attempting to rationalize their failure. At an unprecented South Central Los Angeles hearing, where former CIA director John Deutch fielded questions from an angry audience, former Los Angeles Police Department officer, Michael Ruppert, stood up and charged that: "the CIA is complicit in bringing drugs into this country" and that the Agency had infiltrated the L.A.P.D. Ruppert elaborated on the same charges in a private interview with this writer.

Adding fuel to the flaming anger of community representatives in South Central Los Angeles is the fact that after 28 months behind bars, Danilo Blandon, an admitted supplier of crack to South Central Los Angeles, was hired as a full-time DEA informant, receiving more than $166,000, this according to the Institute of Policy Studies, a Washington, D.C. think tank.

The same think tank quotes U.S. senate investigations that: "the U.S. Attorney in San Francisco returned $36,800 seized from a Nicaraguan drug dealer after two Contra leaders sent letters to the court arguing that the cash was intended for the Contras."

Forget about O.J. Simpson. In South Central Los Angeles, this was the number one story in 1996-97.

With these and other similar stories floating around, African-American Congresswomen Maxine Waters and Juanita Millender-MacDonald, have been conducting their own investigations and insist that crack-based gang violence in their districts was triggered by external forces.

"The most heavily armed teenage gangsters in Los Angeles still belong to the Crips, the federation of young blacks who, with their droopy pants, blue bandannas and hobbling shuffle ... now control the city's lucrative crack trade," according to a late 1995 *Economist* article.

The red-bandanna Bloods are the legendary rivals of the Crips, although there has been an on-and-off truce between the two groups.

The *L.A. Times* reports that the largest gang in Los Angeles is now the Latino 18th Street gang. Latino gangs specialize in selling home-grown narcotics such as marijauna, amphetamines and PCP. Meanwhile, Asian gangs specialize in vehicle hijacking and burglary.

White surfer gangs along the coast are content to control their patch of beach, slitting tires, breaking car windows and physically harrassing intruding surfers.

The Economist establishes a cause-and-effect relationship between the shutting down of foundries and small factories that once provided a living for many young Angelinos and the rise of drug fiefs in the same neighborhoods. "Some researchers reckon that as many as 10,000 gang members in the city can now make their living just from selling crack."

In Compton, the city where I had talked with Bear, an eruption of 12 gang-related shootings was possibly connected to the murder of rap singer Tupac Shakur, and another gang-related death is on the news as I write these lines.

But news events that trigger eruptions of gang violence (the results of a trial, the death of a rap singer), are usually symptoms rather than root causes. These events make it tougher for the real heroes of gang neighborhoods, members of organizations that work directly with gang members. One of many examples of the heroic struggle from within is RAP (Real Alternative Program), based in San Francisco's Mission District, where street murals and bohemian cafes provide a colorful setting for tragic stories.

RAP's four-member Calles Project is literally saving lives by using case managers, diversion, crisis intervention and outreach.

"On certain days we successfully intervene, but other times we're told 'Ray, you better just leave – it's not safe'," says Ray Balberon of RAP.

"It's not being in a gang that's the problem," he says. "For many, that's all the family they have. But we offer choices like nonviolence and responsibility."

San Francisco's primarily Latino Mission District is one of the most exciting places to visit in the U.S.A., for its mural art, historic buildings, and a street life that combines old-fashioned ma-and-pa business with avant-garde bohemians. Yet between 1993 and 1996, 48 Latinos died from gunshot wounds in the Mission District alone.

Like Compton and Pico-Union in L.A. the Mission District will probably look menacing to the outsider who has read the statistics. But attracted by the relatively low rents, poets, painters and alternative theater artists are moving into the neighborhood. These pioneers love their turf, gangs or no gangs.

Some of the most exciting and attractive neighborhoods in California include a gang element. Venice, for example, is to Southern California what the Mission is up north.

"So you're not going to tell me you live in a safe neighborhood," I say to Rick, a long-time Venice Beach resident.

59

"You've got to mind your Ps and Qs wherever you are," he responds. "I'm not saying you wouldn't read about it and think there's a problem. People come from all over. That means that conceivably two guys from rival gangs could cross each other's path. But I love Venice and I'm not going anywhere else."

But Venice and The Mission are the best of neighborhoods with reputations for street violence. In places like Compton or Pico-Union, residents directly affected by gang violence and bound to their "turf" for economic reasons, can't wait for the opportunity to move out, even if to relocate in a monotonous suburb.

IMMIGRANTS AND MEDIEVAL CALIFORNIA

Even if it were advisable to write the typical feel-good account of the immigrant story, like "the Chinese built the railroads," there are too many immigrant groups, more than a hundred depending on how you count them, and too many subculture nuances to accomplish more than a superficial overview.

The Chinese-railroad connection illustrates the dilemma of describing immigrant cultures. To call this a cultural correlation (that the Chinese build railroads) would be nothing less than absurd. Do most Chinese back in China build railroads? In nineteenth-century California, written and unwritten laws dictated what Asian immigrants could and could not do for a living, not much different from the plight of the Jews in medieval Europe. Nineteenth-century California allowed and encouraged the Chinese to work on railroads, so build railroads they did.

The Philippines provide a contemporary example. When one has the misfortune to be decked out in a California hospital room, it's a good bet the orderly or nurse entering the room will be Philippino.

Yet back in the Philippines, it would be statistically impossible for such a high proportion of Philippine people to be nurses or orderlies. In contemporary California, the old medieval guild traditions prevail; certain jobs are set aside for people of certain backgrounds.

In California (and other parts of the U.S.), Greek immigrants have rescued an American tradition: the coffee shop restaurant, which was on the way to becoming extinct with the rise of fast food chains and theme restaurants. A large proportion of coffee shops serving traditional American food are owned and run by Greeks. If this had something to do with Greek culture then I should be able to go to any restaurant in Greece and find a typical American coffee shop, with a bacon and eggs breakfast or a T-bone steak with baked potatoes for dinner.

Unwritten Codes

The traditions that compartamentalize immigrants into specialty jobs are derived from subtle, unwritten codes, but there have been written laws that illustrate the medieval guildlike structure of the ethnic-employment tradition.

From 1951 to 1964, a time when immigration was tightly restricted, millions of Mexicans were lured to California as legal agricultural workers in what was known as the "Bracero Program." Back in Mexico, where I have lived at times, there are many sophisticated architects and auto mechanics, for exampl, but California has never purposely imported architects or auto mechanics from Mexico.

Unwritten codes have followed the pattern of the Bracero Program. In one neighborhood where I lived, several restauranteurs learned that I had Mexican friends. When these entrepreneurs needed kitchen help, they would ask me if I could find them a Mexican.

The Orange Curtain

Disneyland's Orange County has been referred to as "The Orange Curtain." For years, jingoistic Robert Dornan's reelection to U.S. Congress had been considered "a mortal lock" by those who bet on election campaigns. (Former B-1 fighter pilot Dornan once grabbed a fellow congressman by the collar on the floor of Congress and denounced him as a wimp.)

61

In November of 1996, Dornan was defeated by none other than an Hispanic woman, Loretta Sánchez. The influx of immigrants is changing the political complexion of the country. Dornan protested that an immigrant advocacy organization had registered Hispanics to vote who had not yet received their citizenship, thus causing his defeat. The vote tally was close, but the number of questionable votes was not enough to change the result of the election.

Sanchez's victory has been encouraging to California immigrants but successful state election ballot propositions with anti-immigrant nuances suggest that an invisible social curtain yet prevents immigrants as a class from fully integrating in the job market.

Surmounting Barriers

I have interviewed numerous successful immigrants in order to ascertain which tactics are most effective for surmounting social and business barriers. The composite answer seems too simplistic to be true, but it appears that the most effective path to social or employment success is a substantial dose of personal and national pride.

One South American woman, a long-time California resident, suggests that: "especially for immigrants, if you are well dressed, behave politely and *act important*, you're more likely to be treated with dignity."

Visible and Invisible Minorities

California gropes to find a common way for so many peoples of varied backgrounds. The spectrum of attitudes towards multiculturalism ranges from joyous celebration to fear that culture contradictions will forever inhibit a common modality.

The Canadians, recognizing that racism affects some more than others, distinguish between visible minorities, and those white minorities who find it easier to blend in. Somewhere between these two categories is the person who may look like the dominant culture but who speaks with an accent.

California's culture map is especially complex. Its diversity includes minorities who were never immigrants: African-Americans, Native Americans and Chicanos. Mexicans who arrive here, legally or illegally, are returning to a land that was once theirs, and whose street and city names come from the Mexican past. Other immigrants are political refugees, like the fifteen-year-old Salvadoran gang member in San Francisco who handed over a gun to RAP's Ray Balberon.

"The boy who gave me this was suffering from post-traumatic stress because he witnessed the annihilation of his entire village in El Salvador," explained Balberon. "The millions this country sent to El Salvador's death squads are now right in our face."

Then there are invisible immigrants, the Okies, for example, who came in the thirties to escape the dust bowl in the Oklahoma region. California's Okie core is the growing Central Valley city of Bakersfield. Country-western singer Merle Haggard, a legend in the music industry who sang that he was "proud to be an Okie from Muskogee" has forsaken Beverly Hills and remained in unpretentious Bakersfield.

Other less visible minorities predominantly in California include the Armenians, ennobled in the literature of William Saroyan, and the Iranians.

When the Iranian fundamentalists held U.S. Embassy personnel hostage in Teheran during the Jimmy Carter administration in the late seventies, Californian Iranians who had nothing to do with the Ayatollah were suddenly more visible and became the target of sporadic attacks. One Arab American who looked Iranian was bloodied by attackers.

In the early days of the hostage crisis, a new version of the Japanese internment tragedy seemed imminent. But the initial outbreaks of anti-Iranian violence subsided and reason returned.

During the depression, over a million Mexican-Americans from the Southwest, many of whose families had been U.S. citizens for generations, were "deported" to Mexico, a land that many of them had never seen, ostensibly because they looked Mexican. In Cheech Marin's movie "Born in East L.A.," the main character, a Mexican-American (U.S. citizen), is caught without his I.D. in an immigration raid and deported to Mexico, where he feels out of place. He must attempt to return "illegally" to his native city, Los Angeles.

The African-American story in California is a well-kept secret. Three men and one woman of African descent participated in Sir Francis Drake's expedition to California in the 1500s. Some of the Spanish soldiers who came here in the 1700s were black men.

Photo: Siomara Cramer

Aztec Dancers at the Plaza Olvera, Los Angeles.

Although California was admitted to the Union in 1850 as a "Free State," a fugitive slave law meant that enslaved blacks who escaped to California could be returned to their "owners." Lured by the Gold Rush, some escaped blacks took the risk, while others were brought here to search for gold by slaveowners.

In 1851, a black woman named Biddy Mason won a precedent-setting court decision; if a slaveowner stayed in a free state longer than three years, he lost his right to his slaves. Mason became a real estate pioneer and philanthropist in San Bernardino, the desert city east of Los Angeles.

African-Americans have held the highest state, municipal and judicial positions, even though they represent less than 10% of the state's population.

Asian-Pacific residents, another "visible minority," represent nearly 10% of the population. Anglo-Americans represent about 43% of the population while Latinos, the fastest growing sector, are approaching 30% and will surpass the whites by the year 2020. But the Asians, according to an *Economist* article, are the most likely to take over state hegemony from the whites. General population statistics show that Latinos account for only half their expected proportion in freshman university classes. Should voted scalebacks in affirmative action programs survive court appeals, this gap would widen.

The Economist bases its projections on 1994 statistics. On several major California university campuses, Asian students outnumbered whites in freshmen classes. Stanford professor Sanford Dornbusch blames inbalance between Asians and Hispanics on the "tracking" system used in elementary grades, by which teachers classify children early into "low" or "college bound" streams. Others say there is simply too much economic pressure on Latin boys to leave school and take badly paid jobs. Latino children accounted for more than half of the children aged 17 or younger who were living below the official poverty level in California, while Asian children made up only 11%.

BUKOWSKI

Will a foul-mouthed, cantankerous, alcoholic poet get the statue he deserves?

Many Europeans experience California through the iconoclast street literature of Charles Bukowski. Born in Germany, Bukowski was brought to California as a pre-schooler. *Ham on Rye*, the first novel in his chronological existence, begins under a dining table with an unflattered, childs-eye, legs-up description of parents and relatives eating above. As a youth, severe skin problems leave him scarred on the surface and within.

In one passage, Bukowski's stern, working class father forces him to redo a lawn mowing job because some blades of grass were not even with the rest. Bukowski writes in a later poem that his father's only theme of conversation was work, kindling an anti-work ethic in the son.

But for Bukowski to develop his odes against exploitative labor, he first paid his dues, working at various humiliating jobs, epitomized in the novel *Post Office*, where he felt oppressed for many years by bureaucratic, unimaginative postal employers. This novel anticipates by a decade the acts of violence of the now proverbial "disgruntled postal employee."

Within Bukowski's literature it is difficult to differentiate between the writer himself and his persona Henry Chinaski. The literary persona enters the author's real life as his drinking buddies call him Hank.

When living in France, I marveled at Bernard Pivot's *Apostrophes* prime time Friday night TV program in which Bukowski, one of a panel of distinguished literary guests, arrived on stage drunk and proceeded to insult the other guests until he had to be escorted out of the studio by security guards.

The *Apostrophes* marketers used footage as publicity. Bukowski's European sales, which already far exceeded U.S. sales, went through the roof, in what must have been the best unintended publicity stunt since Van Gogh cut off his ear.

Before Charles Bukowski became a well-known writer, a long hiatus in his career found his roominghouse existence divided between various menial jobs and unemployment on the sun-baked streets of Hollywood. Bukowski was a confirmed alcoholic and sometimes homeless poet. His poetry includes barroom brawls and spats with whores but beneath the surface there is a profound, non-sectarian, non-political defense of the downtrodden. There is much pathos in his understated verses on the life of the nightshift laborer.

"Although each night had been long, the years had gone fast," he wrote.

"Bukowski's work," affirms critic Russell Harrison, "everywhere embodies, explicitly or implicitly, a rejection of the ideology of success and power."

Like Cervantes, Bukowski first became marketable after his fiftieth birthday. He developed a following in California, where he remained steadfastly loyal to his small publisher, Black Sparrow Press, and then in Europe, where sales of his books finally gave him some modicum of financial independence. The east coast literary establishment, whose literature often came from the ivory tower of university campuses, continued to ignore Bukowski's captivating page quality, a brutally honest yet subtly stylized literature that sprung from the gritty source of human agony.

Why the affinity with Europe? Lines in a poem "for my ivy league friends," illustrate the east coast-west coast antithesis that binds California psychologically to Europe. (Note: "they" are the east coast literary critics; "the row" refers to alcoholics' "skid row.")

yet their attacks upon me have been effective in this country and
if it weren't for Europe I'd probably still be a starving writer
or down at the row
or diggin weeds out of your garden

(The east-west schism would draw other socially critical writers to California. Poet and novelist Alice Walker, of *The Color Purple* fame, wrote: "In 1978 I moved from Brooklyn, New York, where I'd lived for four years after leaving Mississippi to northern California. It was one of the best decisions I ever made. My spirit, which had felt so cramped on the East Coast, expanded fully ....")

Bukowski would drive by Disneyland on his way to night racing at Los Alamitos race track in Orange County, yet there is nothing about the Disneyland version of California in his literature. The author had lived in the shadow of the Hollywood film industry, but California's greatest icon, its cinema, is belittled by Bukowski:

Sitting there in a seat
among the lonely and
insufficient people,
and the screen flashes
its genius
only it's not there
it misses as it has
almost always missed –
millions of dollars
pissed away.
The people are so used
to being conned

When "Hollywood" reluctantly recognized Bukowski, it was a French director who filmed *Barfly*. The filming of *Barfly* is the theme of a later, more mellow yet humorously critical Bukowski novel called *Hollywood*.

By the nineties, with Bukowski nearing death, a large contingent of his devoted readers, many of whom were writers themselves, wrote narrations of their personal experiences with Bukowski/Chinaski. We read about the times he hurled staggering insults at the audience attending his readings (he only did readings to pay the bills and often arrived to the stage drunk and reluctant).

Lionel Rolfe writes about the "interview" with Bukowski that ended up as a drunken party, an anti-celebration of another movie based on a Bukowski story.

There were even narrations of former Bukowski girlfriends, who claimed they were treated with respect in private only to then read disparaging accounts of their affairs in his poetry. Reading between the lines, one suspects that behind Bukowski's ornery, egotistic, misanthropic persona is another man who deeply cares for others. His love poems to Jane and his stories of solidarity with the outcasts of society are quite stirring.

On one sunlit winter afternoon beneath the San Gabriel Mountains, I had potential bets in the third and seventh races at Santa Anita. I took a book of Bukowski poetry for the nearly two hours I'd have to wait between those races. I sat on the fresh lawn of the infield, looking up towards the grandstand.

There was Bukowski, the loner, at the remote end of the grandstand, where he could have the whole section of seats to himself. I'd seen him often, at the thoroughbreds and the harness races, but I'd never approached him, remembering his anti-social reputation but also respecting the need for concentration when one is making serious betting decisions.

This time, armed with his book, I summoned the courage to walk up to his rows of seats to ask for an autograph.

I had once written a letter to Bukowski, in search of an opinion for a literary article. I never expected a response. But he responded promptly with a "Hell Mark," and gave me a good answer. That was the type of solidarity from one who, alone at the typewriter, had conceived poems that made tormented souls joyful to find a companion in anguish. But how would this sometimes belligerent social persona react in person?

"Hey, Bukowski," I said. "How about an autograph."

He looked up and grinned. He took the book in hand: *The Days Run Away like Wild Horses Over the Hills*.

"Haven't seen this one in a long time!" he said.

In all the times that I'd seen him at the track, he never looked drunk. Horse racing seemed to bring out the best in him. The race track was his refuge.

69

We shook hands and wished each other luck on the day's card. Back in the infield, I opened the book and read his inscription. "Well, shit, I had the 4. O. K. Hails, Charles Bukowski."

Accompanying the inscription was a typical Bukowski self-caricature.

Bukowski's death brought no sorrow because he had lived a fertile and intense life, the last half of which was spent doing what he loved, writing and playing the horses. His relationships with women seemed to mellow like an aging wine and his last wife, as portrayed in *Hollywood*, was a true companion.

The old Volkswagen and the dirty rooming houses had been ditched in favor of a BMW and a nice house in the working class suburb of San Pedro, where there were no other writers around. His cast-iron stomach had taken in all that wine and booze, yet his liver had held up. He died of leukemia.

Here in California, many nonconformist lives have been enriched by the existence of Charles Bukowski. But the devoted Bukowski following does not develop into a cult; his followers are too individualistic.

People don't talk too much to strangers around here. If I carry a Hemingway or a Steinbeck, no one comes up and shakes my hand. But in California when a stranger sees me with a Bukowski book in hand, it's odds-on he becomes an instant friend. The literature of the anti-social persona Hank Chinaski has created human bonds he never would have imagined!

The bureaucrats who decide which dead people get monuments will never commission a statue of Charles Bukowski, and it is better that way. How can you create an icon out of an iconoclast?

CELEBRITIES AND THE HOMELESS

In structuring a protrayal of characters of California, I groped for a rational format. I considered working from the bottom up, beginning with the homeless, a phenomenon of human geography since they are attracted to California's benign climate, and ending with wealthy celebrities, another California phenomenon nurtured by the film and record industries.

During a bizarre period of my life I found myself mingling simultaneously with both of these prototypes. I began to suspect that these opposites, the homeless and celebrities, had something in common.

I would go from a minimum wage position at a printing factory to an interpreting job for government officials and industrialists. It was grimy work at the print shop. On one occasion, I left work without time to clean up, and stuck out my thumb to hitch a ride home, where I would prepare for my other life. An attractive woman in a Porsche picked me up. I entered her car looking like a haggard street person.

She was thrilled to meet a down-and-out Ph.D. She invited me that night to drinks at the exclusive Los Angeles Athletic Club. I must have

71

been intended as a rebellious message to the elite. The conversation that night, at the bar, was no more challenging than the sessions I'd had with winos at bus stop benches.

I was getting to know all kinds of down-and-outers, yet I was also mixing with the cream of the crop in Los Angeles society.

Theories abound as to why people become homeless: substance abuse, low self-esteem, severe physical and psychological battle scars from the Vietnam War, the most porous social net in the developed world, suburbanization and subsequent loss of communities that would provide spontaneous support for their own misfits, and the geographic mobility that contributes to the breakup of the traditional extended family.

Sometimes, it gets more complex. Was Bukowski's period of homelessness alcohol-driven, or a rebellion against the ideology of success and power? I met two homeless men who hung out at one of the prettier places in California, a green park on Temescal Canyon Road overlooking the Will Rogers Beach. They were apparently not alcoholics, for their drink of preference was coffee, which they brewed with the electric outlet of the public men's room.

In the hobo tradition, these guys would take occasional odd jobs, just enough for food and clothing, and then hang out and laugh at the rat race around them. But these gentlemen were the atypical elite of the homeless.

Increasingly, with cuts in social services, whole families are becoming homeless. If you've got kids to support, a minimum wage can't pay the rent. For the most part, homeless people I've encountered up and down the coast of California tend to be self-destructive in one way or another.

At the same time I was able to observe a large dose of self-destructiveness among L.A.'s elite. Each Friday afternoon, I watched the famous president of a law firm (where I did translating) snort cocaine; during the week, his team of secretaries and clerks covered for his irresponsibility.

During Spanish/English interpreting excursions with politicians and industrialists, I could not keep up with the frenetic drinking, which began with morning cocktails and ended late at night after formal dinners. There were occasions when a mayor I worked for was so bogged down by drink that he'd say: "Mark, you know what I need to say; you go up there and give that speech for me."

My first-hand experiences on both ends of the social spectrum have led to a hypothesis: the main difference between the homeless on the bottom and the celebrities on the top is luck. A few years after my own experience, the film *Trading Places* made a similar point.

Greg Smith, who operates Grave Line tours, agrees that "amongst the stars one finds the common denominator of everyone." Smith's two-hour tawdry tour takes you to "the seamiest sites of the City of Sins, Hollywood's Babylon at its most unflattering angle. It's an information orgy as you cruise by over 75 sites of celluloid deaths! Sins! Scandals!"

Is Smith's hearse-driven tour to death sites another example of Hollywood tabloidism? Just the opposite, he responds. He is a professional researcher with an enormous data base on the lives of famous L.A. people. "The last breath locations of legendary luminaries," he suggests, provide a more honest rendering of celebrity reality than the typical Tinseltown tour.

Drug addiction among the homeless is thus a counterpoint for the California OD deaths of Janis Joplin, John Belushi, River Phoenix and others. Some of the other features of Grave Line Tours: "Errol Flynn raped a 17-year-old here; Hugh Grant's brush with the divine; José and Kitty Menendez murder home; Richard Dreyfuss cracks-up car on coke ..." and much more.

Grave Line Tours, a take-off on the stodgy Gray Line Tours, departs at 9:30 am from the corner of Hollywood Boulevard and Orchid in pre-1976 hearses, the big ones that were discontinued after the gas crisis. (For reservations, phone toll-free 1-800-797-DEAD or locally at 213-469-4149, for these magical misery tours that cost $40.)

A sports car provides a resting place for this homeless man.

Meanwhile, California authorities tend to be tougher on the homeless than on the parallel self-destructive behavior of the elite. San Francisco has attempted to implement a controversial Matrix program, with massive sweeps of homeless people from parks and neighborhoods and a curfew at Golden Gate Park. Police squads on horseback and motorcycles conducted dawn raids in city parks, rousing the homeless from sleep.

Jennifer Wolch and Michael Dear, geography professors at the University of Southern California, authors of the 1993 book *Malign Neglect: Homelessness in an American City*, assert that the attack on the welfare state at all levels of government has had serious conse-quences for the most vulnerable populations. Not only did California fail to compensate for the effects of federal retrenchment but state tax revolts of the 1970s resulted in even more drastic cutbacks. Wolch and Dear found that landlords were often unwilling to rent to families receiving welfare benefits.

The authors refer to NIMBYism (Not In My Back Yard) in Venice, California, where homeowners and merchants in a slow-growth coalition allied with their opponents, pro-development realtors and investors, to support a growing repressiveness and hostility toward homeless people.

The authors describe a paradox. A strong community of homeless people can both be an important resource that enables many to survive, as well as a hindrance for those trying to move out of homelessness.

Visitors to California motivated to do volunteer work may read stories to homeless children, serve in a soup kitchen, or engage in activities related to rehabilitation. For more information, call San Francisco's Coalition on Homelessness at 415-346-9693, or ask for James at Chrysalis in Los Angeles, at 213-895-7777.

In August of 1995, in characteristic San Francisco style, homeless activists in the Bay Area invaded the mayor's affluent Pacific Heights neighborhood, mocking the "Take Back the Parks" initiative of the Matrix Program with chants of "Take Back Pacific Heights."

"The problem is not homelessness," responded then Mayor Jordan, but behavioral problems … their unacceptable, unhealthy lifestyle shouldn't be forced on the neighbors."

Down in Southern California, the Chrysalis program, with branches in Downtown's skid row, Santa Monica, and Hollywood, is more practical, finding jobs for the homeless. The apparent gap between film celebrities and the homeless is bridged by Mara Manus, founder of Chrysalis, herself a refugee from the film industry.

Chrysalis is a non-profit employment service, providing an address and phone number for homeless job seekers, a fax machine, computers for resumés, and guidance through mock interviews.

"On skid row we deal with mostly single males," says Ed Hennessey of Chrysalis. "But our Santa Monica office serves about 50% females."

The Chrysalis batting average is impressive. "In 1996," says Hennessy, "1,700 people came through our skid row office, and 536 of them are now working."

Hennessey believes that low self-esteem is the most under-addressed problem within the homeless community, and that the extraordinary encarceration rate in the United States is exacerbating the problem.

After taking a Grave Line Tour, one wonders about the differences between the self-destructivenes of the Hollywood elite and the homeless.

"Celebrities have something to fall back on," says Ed Hennessy of the Chrysalis program. "They can go to the Betty Ford Clinic and clean up. The difference is, when you've hit rock bottom, who's there to help you out?"

When I wrote *Culture Shock! Bolivia*, I faced the dilemma of how to advise readers to deal with beggars in one of the poorer nations in the world. Now, in the richest state of the richest nation in the world, I face the same dilemma!

My daughter Siomara just returned from volunteer work amongst the homeless in downtown L.A. One of the men she met had been reading a book. He held it up.

"This book's got everything," he said. "I recommend it."

It was a dictionary.

SURFING CULTURE AND THE BIG CORPORATE WAVE

Ian Blair has surfed on most of the beaches along the California coast and returns to his home state to ride the waves whenever he can take leave of his New York publishing job. The culture is changing, Blair laments.

"Now people arrive in their expensive cars. Guys used to drive old crapped-out Mercury Station Wagons and used to sleep in their cars.

"Now a whole corporate surf culture has developed. Companies that started with surf trolls in swim trunks are now on the stock exchange, mainly in Orange County.

"I'm totally against that. I'm enough of a self-righteous jerk to tell others, that's no good. Forget the fact that they're paying kids in Asia 12 cents an hour to sew swim trunks."

Orange County and part of San Diego County, Blair says, is the "nerve center of major surfboard and apparel companies, as well as surfing magazines. Northern California still offers more breathing room but if you're not a local up there, you can feel an unpleasant vibe."

Has Blair ever been harassed by surfer gangs?

"Just once, at a place called Stockton Avenue. As I was waxing my board, guys on the cliff were throwing rocks at me. The surfer magazines, when they have a picture of this place, they'll give it a pseudonym, like Weasel Beach, so people can't find it."

The Lunada Bay gang, on the exclusive peninsula of Palos Verdes, south of L.A. are known as the Bay Boys. They are infamous for their hostility toward newcomers. The Bay Boys have welcomed outsiders by slashing their tires, smashing windows, stoning, and even shooting at them with pellet guns.

Writer Michael Goodman calls the Bay Boys the "Coastal Nostra." One of the local surfers asked Goodman to "keep writing that this is a war zone …. We don't like riffraff comin' up here."

The Bay Boys describe themselves as a "brotherhood," big on hazing, with banishment as the ultimate punishment.

"Racially," writes Goodman, "the Bay Boys are an accurate reflection of the wealthy whiteness of their manicured and gated peninsula." A prerequisite for membership is having lived or grown up in Palos Verdes Estates, which overlooks Lunada Bay.

At this writing, there is a pending civil suit filed by seven Torrence surfers, including Hagan Kelley, a national amateur champion. Kelley had received death threats after starting to surf in the bay.

Local Palos Verdes police were providing only minimal protection for outside surfers on this public beach, suggesting that the surfers are pawns in an effort to maintain the exclusive nature of the community.

One local surfer told the *L.A. Times* that they protect their beach for a purpose. "The crowds are so intense, you can't have your own little sanctuary. But we do."

My cousin George, also a devoted surfer, has had his windows smashed at another beach in the Los Angeles basin; the Bay Boys and the Stockton Avenue crowd are not the only menace to outsiders.

But Blair thinks the greater menace is the corporatization of his subculture. He fears that adding surfing to the Olympic Games might once and for all ruin the sport.

For the time being, the California coast continues to offer a rich surfing experience. Ian Blair's two favorite surfing spots are quite different from each other.

"Big Sur River mouth has everything in terms of aesthetics," he affirms with joy. "You're looking back to the shore upon the pristine, unspoiled Santa Lucia Mountains, instead of looking at McDonalds, condos or traffic lights. There's a campground on the meadow near Big Sur River, near where Henry Miller had his cabin."

Photo: Greg Pio

Great surfing near Santa Cruz.

Blair's other favorite spot is Steamer Lane, near Santa Cruz.

"Steamer Lane is a microcosm of how surfing has changed since the 70s. Before you could paddle out there and you knew everyone around you. Now it's a total body jam. Even when you get up at dawn, there's the crack-of-dawn crowd.

"Yes, it's crowded, but it's got consistent waves. Any nearby swell at all and this place will have the best waves. It's also a neat place to watch people surf. The cliff around the bay forms a natural amphitheatre."

Ian Blair, who has lived and worked in both New York and his native California, will be back in the next chapter to express his views on business and social customs as they differ from coast to coast. New and unique characters will be introduced. Contrastive analysis will delve into three distinct layers of culture clash: Northern and Southern California, California and the East Coast, and foreigners in California.

— Chapter Four —

MAPPING SOCIAL AND BUSINESS CUSTOMS

We now arrive within a three-dimensional map of California. Horizontally, it shows regional nuances. Vertically, it exposes a cross-section of customs. Beneath the dominant way of life are layers of coexisting cultures, emerging and receding throughout the California story. The instability of these layers periodically flares up into culture quakes.

In California, corporate conformism, iconoclast rebelliousness, regional differences, and immigrant traditions weave a contradictory texture of social and business customs.

Such a complex social landscape requires more than one writer's perspective. An eclectic array of perceptive observers are called upon, some of whom arrived in California from other parts of the U.S.A. or from abroad to experience their own version of culture shock.

Without attempting to sift out any one great truth, examples in this chapter, laid out in the spirit of California's outdoor murals, should help make sense of the multicultural landscape.

SOUTH AND NORTH

Isn't it nice that people who prefer Los Angeles to San Francisco live there?
—Herb Caen, San Francisco's most beloved columnist

The primary California contrast is between Northern (San Francisco Bay Area Hub) and Southern, whose core is the Los Angeles basin.

"When I first moved to Los Angeles," writes consumer travel expert Peter S. Greenberg, "it took me 10 years to really learn my way around. When I later moved to San Francisco, it took me just three weeks to figure it all out.

"It's not that San Francisco is simple – it's that San Francisco makes sense. Yes, I'll admit that compared to New York, San Francisco could be described as a boutique city. But the real beauty of San Francisco is that as proud of the city as its people are … they don't erect any barriers to visitors."

Like Greenberg, author and publisher Mike Helm has lived and worked in both the south (the San Fernando Valley) and the north (San Francisco and Berkeley). He opted for the north.

"Southern California is the land of the fast buck and the hard sell. Insincerity is an art form down in Hollywood. Up here there's the pretention of being laid back but the people who run Northern California are not the hippies, even though there's a freedom of expression."

Helm believes that natural surroundings play a role in north-south cultural differences. "The natural environment, its diversity and beauty, influence people in a more positive way in Northern California."

Novelist Carol Wolpert adresses Helm's critique of Hollywood sincerity. The day after an actor accidently shot and killed himself, an actress had a picture framed of him prominently displayed on her coffee table. People believe that they can benefit from "clout by association" which she calls "Trickle-down cachet." A typical line, satirized by Wolpert: "I met this girl who knows this guy who works for Stallone."

Computer specialist and actor Gene Murray has lived in both north and south, and perceives that "self-image consciousness" in Southern California is not the exclusive domain of Hollywood hopefuls like Wolpert's actress friend. People want to be "perceived as politically correct whereas up north they're correct by nature." ("Politically correct" is a term coined by conservatives to label multiculturalists and social progressives.)

"But now it seems as if the image thing is creeping up north," adds Murray.

Mike Helm also senses that the cultural borders between north and south are beginning to fade. "The differences are not as great as they used to be but here (Bay Area) someone could show up at a business meeting with expensive jeans whereas you'd need a suit for a similar occasion in Southern California.

"Here there's a legacy of the sixties and of gay culture," adds Helm, "more of an insistence of respect for individual presentation. But you still have to take a shower."

In the publishing business, Helm is in a position to call the shots and dress informally. But Bob Roberts, a San Francisco architect, suggests that business etiquette in the Bay Area is guided by no dominant culture, with a sometimes confusing variety of options.

"Some small businesses are uncharacteristically formal," he says, "while employees at a big bank like Wells Fargo might go to work with tattoos and earings."

Roberts agrees with Helm and Murray that the differences between north and south are diminishing, in part because "the movie industry is now involved up here, fusing in with the CD Rom culture of Silicon Valley," just south of the Bay Area.

Bob's girlfriend Kathy agrees that San Francisco is no longer as protective against outsiders, but senses distinct subtexts between south and north.

"In L.A., there's a "waiting-to-be-discovered subtext," she says. "People are expecting the dream to materialize."

(Image of Sunset Boulevard in L.A. "We're trying too hard," writes Tom Huth. "An old red sedan keeps cruising past outdoor cafes of Sunset Plaza, slowing down and honking, calling attention to the boxcar lettering across its side: ACTOR DENNIS WOODRUFF SEEKS HIS BIG BREAK. We're all hustling.")

"The great difference of San Francisco," continues Kathy, "is its overt acknowledgment of same sex relationships."

Kathy and Bob agree that San Francisco has European pretentions and would have liked to be a sister city with Paris, where preservation of great architecture is a prevailing image. San Francisco is more conscious than Los Angeles of preservation because its Victorian architecture demands to be preserved, and the gays, double-income-no-kids "dinks," are well-positioned economically to gentrify old neighborhoods.

Los Angeles, on the other hand, got started much later as a city, so there is less to preserve, and newness is more a part of the ideology.

We've already met Ian Blair through his commentary on the surfer culture.

"The Southern California thing is a little more flashy, happy-go-lucky," Ian explains. "People up in Northern California can get a little more parochial. They don't want the Disney Corporation coming in."

Disagreeing in nuance with both Helm and Roberts, Blair says that, "I probably would feel a little more free, in a strange way, in Southern California, where people just want to make a buck and leave you alone. In the North, people want to keep the invading hordes out."

83

People who "just want to make a buck and leave you alone" need no sense of community. Blair is not the first to insinuate that Northern Californians want to keep their good thing in their own neighborhood. But Greenberg implies that the greater sense of community in Northern California does not exclude outsiders.

"Within a month" (of moving to San Francisco) I knew every one of my neighbors on a first-name basis. I knew the shopkeepers, and at some restaurants, after my second visit, I didn't have to order – they knew what I wanted."

Greenberg was simply practising the technique that has worked well for me in Paris: do business at the same places until they get to know you. You can do this in the San Francisco Bay area, which is much nearer to France than L.A. in psychic geography.

They are trying to duplicate the European cafe culture in Southern California. At the Java coffee house in Newhall, I've already filled three pink cards with stamps of purchase and gotten three free coffees and they still don't know me. In Paris, in the Twentieth Arrondissement, I would sit down at a table in my preferred no-name cafe. The bartender knew what I wanted, and brought it to me without my asking – ever since my third visit.

At Java 'n Jazz they've got 15 varieties of cafe, latte, capuccino, espresso, hazelnut …, and they've got sofas upstairs for a living-room atmosphere. In France, espresso is just called cafe, and you can have it black or au lait, standing at the zinc counter or paying an extra franc or two to sit outside.

L.A. thinks it can now rival Paris in cafe culture. But with fifteen different part-time employees here at Java 'n Jazz, all of them overtly friendlier than my bartender in Paris, you could come here for the rest of your life and still remain anonymous.

Does geography influence culture, as suggested by John McKinney and Mike Helm? In hilly, unpredictable neighborhoods of L.A. like Silver Lake and Echo Park, places that bear a greater resemblance to San Francisco, one is more likely to feel a sense of community and the personal attention that comes with it. Hills define boundaries of neighborhoods in Silver Lake and Echo Park. They are like patches of San Francisco in Los Angeles.

A superb public transportation system in San Francisco gives that city's neighborhoods an advantage, removing folks from their cars and placing them on the streets.

Native San Franciscan and journalist Louis H. Lapham came to the defense of Los Angeles when he was assigned to participate in a stereotypical photo essay which was to label L.A. the "Athens of the West."

"Not only was it wrong," he analyzes, "it was monstrous heresy …. They (San Franciscans) flatter themselves on their sophistication, their exquisite sensibility, their devotion to the arts. Los Angeles represents (to them) the antithesis of these graces; it is the land of the Philistines, lying somewhere to the south in the midst of housing developments that stand as the embodiment of ugliness, vulgarity, and corruptions of the spirit."

Everyone has their opinion of the cultural differences between north and south. We've sought out opinions of people who lived in both regions of California. Their views are sometimes contradictory. No one said that California culture is easily defined.

WEST AND EAST

I mean, who would want to live in a place where the only cultural advantage is that you can turn right on a red light?
—New Yorker Woody Allen, referring to L.A.

It's a scientific fact that if you stay in California you lose one point of your IQ every year.
—Eastern writer Truman Capote

Living in California adds ten years to a man's life. And those extra ten years I'd like to spend in New York.
—Harry Ruby

In his "California Rising," Wallace Stegner referred to what he perceived as a New York bias in the publishing society. "American writing is done everywhere," he wrote in 1981. "A lot of it, and some of the best, is done in California." But the publishing industry is done pretty much in Manhattan. In the New York book reviews, "California as often as not is embarrassed to find itself pictured as grotesque or trivial."

Stegner admits that California has produced a lot of screwballs, and laments that "all Californians may be tainted by association. In a notably free and exuberant society, nearly anything goes, and sometimes it goes sour. But I think it is not California's failures and excesses that have bred antagonism in the east. Success has more to do with it. Emotions – simple, direct, and understandable are at work. Envy and fear."

Mostly we hear of native New Yorkers migrating to California.

Ian Blair, our surfer-publisher friend went the other way, from California to New York. Unlike Stegner, he is not as quick to defend his native California.

"I'll quote a famous cliche," Ian said. "In California people say, 'Have a nice day' and they really mean, 'Fuck you.' In New York they say, 'Fuck you' and they really mean, 'Have a nice day.' It's nothing personal in New York. You can do it to them too. You can give it to people with both barrels.

"In the California veneer of sunshine and daydreams, everybody wants to be self-actualized. It's a much more confrontational culture in New York, but healthier because it's good to confront things. In California you're more likely to get stabbed in the back."

Kathy moved in the opposite direction from Ian, brought up in New York and today residing in San Francisco. She offers a kinder picture of California.

"In New York, people live to work. They want to like their work. In California, people live to play. They work so that they can play."

Karl, originally from Germany, came to the United States after having worked for years in London. He arrived on the east coast, and worked there until he landed a university teaching job in the pharmaceutical field in Los Angeles. Karl agrees with Kathy.

"Back east, people take their work more seriously. Here, they work so that they can have a good time."

The parallel conclusions of Karl and Kathy seem too neat and crisp. Yet both are perceptive observers and neither is prone to cliche. Clearly there are great cultural contrasts between New York and California. But what are they and why do they exist?

"New York attitudes kind of mirror New York geography: the closed-in feeling in the east, the wide open scenery in the west," hypothesises Gene Murray. But geography and culture are not independent variables.

"In New York, ideas, if they're not based on some sort of tradition, make people skeptical," Murray explains. "In hands-off California, *you* think what *you* want to and *I* think what *I* want."

Amy Carter, in her twenties, compares California with the east in the social and intellectual realm, from the perspective of one who had lived in a Washington D.C. urban suburb and had spent a year in Paris before going to study "behind the Orange Curtain" at California State University at Irvine, an Orange County school, whose vast majority of students are locals.

"I was shocked and horrified at the incredible level of materialism, the complete focus of the material over the intellectual or the spiritual. I had a hard time making friends."

Carter is an engaging young woman in her mid-twenties whose sparkling vitality and deep social commitment had attracted a broad array of friends in both France and Washington. Orange County university life was not as kind to her.

"One friend I did have drove a cute convertible Mustang. She once said casually, 'When I turned sixteen, I told my parents it was either a mustang or a jeep.'

"Where I come from," Amy said, "there was never any question of being given a car. The U.C. Irvine parking lot resembled a Lexus dealership. Parents bribed their children to go to college nearby in Irvine with a fancy car."

CALIFORNIA AND THE WORLD

I'm not into those foreign dances.
—Kato Kaelin, O.J. Simpson's houseguest, on Bosnia.

"I wasn't in college in France so this may not be a perfect comparison," Amy continued, "but people there tended to have a grip on current events. The big difference was the political apathy in Orange County and Southern California in general. I remember there was the Bosnian crisis. At Irvine, when you started to talk about anything beyond the borders of the U.S., you just got a blank stare."

Dr. Nigel Sylvester, a former professor at the University of Southern California, agrees with Amy. Comparing California to his native England, Sylvester was surprised to see a place where so many people had gone to a university.

"But it didn't seem like they knew much about the world outside of their specialty," he said. "Young university people in England and Mexico (where Nigel had lived) know much more about the world than their counterparts in California."

New Yorkers and Washingtonians skip across the Atlantic Ocean and arrive in Europe. Californians cross the Pacific and reach Hawaii. Are New Yorkers and Washingtonians nearer to what is happening abroad? Or is the United States passing through a phase of provincialism?

Within California, there are pockets and regions where international consciousness is high, just as there are in the east. Distribution of foreign films, for example, is largely limited to a few hip or counterculture neighborhoods. One would have to ask the distributors if they are responding to levels of interest in the marketplace or manipulating the marketplace for their own purposes.

Foreign visitors coming to California will probably enhance their adjustment and integration if they choose a neighborhood where film distributors send foreign movies.

DESERT MADNESS AND CULTS

City Boy Eaten by Desert Vultures. Desert Pedestrian Run Down by Off-Road Vehicle. Body of New Yorker Found Dehydrated, Clenching Joshua Tree. I imagined these tabloid headlines as I moved into my new spread on the high desert of California, Antelope Valley north of Los Angeles.

It was an irresistible opportunity: live rent free in exchange for caretaking a ranch. Keep the fruit trees watered and you can sell the apricots, peaches and pears. Grow your own vegetables. Raise your own animals. A romantic's back-to-nature dream or a city boy's nightmare?

I planned an experiment for raising hens and pigs on recycled food. The theory came from an old buddy who ran a farmers' market; it takes many more acres of grain growing to feed livestock than it does to feed human beings. Land is more efficiently used by growing produce. I wanted my meat, but felt that I had to produce it in a sustainable way.

Not many deserts are found in the U.S.A. The California high and low deserts are among the few that were not subjected to nuclear testing. Some desert regions of California have unexpectedly rich soil. Southern California legally pilfers its water from the northern part of the state. With sufficient water and no nuclear fallout, this edge of the Mojave was ideal for my experiment.

But how to sell fruit and produce? With my meagre production, supermarkets would not give me the time of day. My operation would be too small for a Department of Agriculture license. (The DOA supplied me with several free how-to booklets.)

Multicultural Support

This particular desert is only fifty miles from Korean and other ethnic grocers in the northern part of L.A., ma-and-pa enterpreneurs willing to buy from small producers.

Multicultural L.A. also afforded me a source of "recycled" food for my hens and pigs. You'll never get a Denny's Restaurant manager to save leftover restaurant food in five-gallon cans, but homespun Salvadoran restaurant owners and Mexican tortilla factory managers were glad to help me out, in exchange for the innards of slaughtered pigs.

The convergence of favorable physical and cultural geographic traits would make this the ideal setting for my experiment.

My do-it-yourself California dream was based on what author Deanne Stillman considers a Mojave desert cultural trait: "the obsessive cultivation of the bedrock of American character – personal rights." But such self-sufficient individualism, as it related to my experiment, would be hardly possible in modern times, but for the existence of an underground, immigrant-nurtured economy.

Desert Individualism

Stillman also refers to this desert as "the land of make-believe." Not far from my spread, Aldous Huxley had experimented with psychedelic drugs, writing his *Doors of Perception*. Too blind to drive in L.A., the desert afforded him the freedom to get behind the wheel without human obstacles.

A few miles up the road, another individualist rebel and one of Vaclav Havel's favorite composers, Frank Zappa, went to high school and began his career of dadaistic rock music and zany art forms. Zappa's music of satire predated the Beatles "Sergeant Pepper's Lonely Heart Club Band." The title of his second album, "Absolutely Free," fits perfectly with the California desert culture. Zappa, an avid defender of First Amendment rights, never condoned the limited American political mold. The essential polarity of politics was "not a matter of conservative vs. liberal but of fascism vs. freedom."

Ah, the freedom of the Mojave desert, where one man's liberty is another man's oppression. They don't heed the speed limit here. I drive within the legal 65 miles an hour; I get tailgaited and must move over for the guy going 85. Whoosh, he passes – and it was a woman. The next one is coming up at 90.

Automobile freedom! The blind Huxley can drive if he wants to, even when high on LSD. Off-road vehicles cut paths where only donkeys and humans should tread. Am I the fascist, believing that this type of freedom is pure craziness? Out on a desert path, I find an old beer can clinging to a sagebrush, a potato chip wrapper skipping in the breeze.

Forget LSD. The natural psychadelic experience up here is the profusion of wildflowers, featuring the golden poppy, from mid-March to mid-May, after the snows have thawed. (An interpretive center is found at the Antelope Valley California Poppy Preserve: 805-765-3533.)

There's a brilliant flash of orange behind the stark foothills beyond my garden. I wonder about the equation between desert and freedom. I've been here for months now and hardly know my neighbors. Is freedom connected with Stegner's "space not place" concept? Do "personal rights" mean that everybody just keeps to themselves, and to their auomobiles?

The Desert: Fertile Ground for the Growth of Cults

This "land of make-believe" has been playing games with me. The total silence of the sunset and the glaring emptiness of noon seem to fertilize metaphysical thought. Three great Western religions were born in the desert. Down below in the basin that extends from San Diego through Los Angeles, before the days of cheap water, this same desert had sloped all the way to the sea. On the coastal semi-desert, today masked by counterfeit greenery, a plethora of cults originated, as described superbly in Carey McWilliams' *Southern California: An Island in the Sun*.

California has been a breeding ground for weird cults. The prototype was Aimee McPherson, founder of the Four Square Gospel: conversion, physical healing, the second coming and redemption.

For McPherson, "Los Angeles was the happy hunting ground for the physically disabled and the mentally inexacting ... no other large city contains so many transplanted villagers who retain the stamp of their indigenous soil," wrote McWilliams.

Here in the desert, I too was a transplanted villager, having come from an old neighborhood in New York where you knew your neighbors and everything was within walking distance. I was now lost in this "space not place."

On May 18, 1926 Sister Aimee disappeared. She was last seen on the beach. Her thousands of faithful followers concluded that she had drowned. A few days later, they collected $35,000 dollars at a great memorial meeting at her Sister of Angelus Temple.

Three days later, she reappeared across the border in Mexico.

Her second coming was hailed with jubilation in Los Angeles, even after her fictitious kidnapping story was disclosed to be false by snoopy reporters.She retained her following but never recovered from the vicious campaign against her and died in 1945 from an overdose of sleeping powder.

"She had an enormous fascination for the uprooted, unhappy, dispirited *lumpenproletariat*," wrote McWilliams. With my own space-not-place alienation, a limping, bearded guru stumbling onto my spread would have easily recruited me as a follower.

The Experiment

At least my experiment was going well. The pigs required minimal amounts of special feed, but gained weight from recycled *burritos* and *pupusas*. Mine may have been the first pigs in California history to appreciate hot *salsa*. The rugged hens loved the leftover tortillas.

There were a few mistakes along the way. The goat I'd purchased to eat the weeds, had been a young girl's pet. To my chagrin, he was a picky eater. Even when I gave him regular feed, the gourmet goat picked out what he liked and left the rest untouched.

Out of ignorance, I'd failed to castrate my male pig while he was manageably small. Pork meat is ruined by male hormones. At the feed store they recommended a local resident who would charge me a moderate sum for castrating the pig, as long as I held him down. At sundown, the event lasted a few moments (long moments for the squealing pig), but thanks to the local anesthetic, the pink pig was up and scampering about in a few minutes. It took me much longer to recover.

I had a soft spot for this male pig because a smaller roan female would push him around. I'd dump their sludgy leftovers into the long feed bin and the female would push the male away with her grunting head.

I added a second bin at the other end of the corral for the male. I'd feed the female first. As she chomped away, she'd peer back, see her partner eating too, and run over to push him away from *his* feed. He'd then scamper to the female's bin, and the process would repeat itself. I sold her at a profit and kept the male for slaughter.

On a diet of recycled food my remaining pig took 6 1/2 months to reach the slaughter weight. Industrial pigs take only five months. With my system he enjoyed an extra month and a half of feasting.

More dilemmas followed. I'd never realized so much fruit could come from apricot trees. The peach and pear trees were prolific as well. The fruit matured faster than I could pick it. The speed at which one must pick fruit in order to make the enterprise profitable was beyond my physical capabilites. Not many citizens would be willing to relocate to the middle of nowhere and pick fruit at assemply-line velocity beginning at the crack of dawn. Were illegal immigrants taking such jobs away from willing Americans?

I'd fill up grocery bags, equivalent to the "lugs" sold to markets, and sell them to Korean grocers. I dried the apricots, first on the wind-swept cement patio, then in the oven. I tried recipes: apricot omelets and apricot chicken. The apricots fell faster than I could pick them. I gave lots of them to the pigs. Antioxidants for a longer life.

The hens were the easiest to take care of, although my two Araucanas (Chilean hens who lay green eggs) managed to fly out above the wire enclosure, hide their nests in the chaparral that the goat had refused to eat, and eventually get killed by wild coyotes. I'd learned how to humanely slaughter the critters from my old L.A. Mexican neighbors.

Fresh brown eggs and fresher chickens were appreciated as dinner gifts more than a bottle of Cabernet-Sauvignon.

My high desert days ended on high and low notes. The high: a brilliant harvest of my modest broccoli field. The low: after a two-week vacation, I discovered that the house I was supposed to caretake had been vandalized. Nothing stolen, but a few windows broken, kitchen utensils and clothing strewn around. Someone had shot through the lens of my camera with a BB gun.

I had lived in the gang-infested Pico-Union neighborhood, and never been victimized by crime. But here, in the lily white high desert, a safe haven for retired L.A.P.D. officers, they'd violated the sanctity of my home.

"In the desert," Stillman writes, "there is little distinction between personal rights and giving in to impulses."

The Mojave Desert was once an ocean. If there had been a beach around here, the local rowdies could have gotten their kicks at the sea. But here they were overwhelmed in waves of emptiness, and the house I was caretaking was a place where they could express their First Amendment rights, letting me know in this eloquent manner that there was no room for a city boy in the empty desert. Did Zappa's "Absolutely Free" mean the right to run wild?

What we needed around here, I thought, was a strong cult leader, an Aimee McPherson, to stitch a purposeful community into the fabric of solitude.

I was able to transplant my Mojave experience to South Central L.A., where I experimented with urban agriculture; a "moveable feast." Beverly Hills residents and suburban zoning zealots would surely object to urban animal raising in their neighborhoods, but here, there were no objections from Mexican and Salvadoran neighbors who were used to that sort of thing. My high-desert experiment had been made possible by the presence of restaurant and grocery owners from traditional cultures.

Some years after leaving my South-Central neighborhood, several nearby retail blocks were burned down in the L.A. riots, including the Korean grocery store where I'd sold my apricots.

CULTURE QUAKE! CALIFORNIA

Most Korean Americans call the 1992 L.A. riots *Sa-i-gu-p'oktong* (4-2-9-riot). The rock throwing, burning and looting began in South Central Los Angeles and spread to other parts of the city after an all-white jury acquitted four officers from the Los Angeles Police Department on charges relating to the severe beating of African-American Rodney King.

Korean small businesses were one of the primary targets in the 1992 uprising.

Blue Dreams: Korean Americans and the Los Angeles Riots (1995) was written by Nancy Abelmann, a fluent speaker of Korean, and John Lie, born in Seoul. Both are University of Illinois professors and experts on Korean culture. The color associated with dreams, hopes, and aspirations in Korea is blue.

"For many Korean Americans," the authors write, "especially the looted merchants, the L.A. riots shattered their faith in the United States and the American dream for which they left their homeland.

In a few days, the material embodiment of their dreams virtually went up in flames ... To be sure, Korean American entrepreneurs did not seek sun and surf in Los Angeles; yet they relentlessly pursued their rendition of the American dream."

Ironically, it was a South Korean made car driven by Rodney King as he was pursued in the high speed chase leading to his beating, and King had a prior arrest for having robbed a Korean-American owned store.

In *Caught in the Middle: Korean Communities in New York and Los Angeles*, author Pyong Gap Min argues that Korean merchants find themselves "caught in the middle" between white wholesalers, landlords and government agencies on the one hand and black customers on the other.

But there is a larger picture in South Central Los Angeles and nearby Koreatown. African-American workers in South Central suffered disproportionately from deindustrialization. Black middle class flight to the suburbs further depressed the area economically. Historically, the phenomenon of immigrant merchants serving minority neighborhoods was nothing new. Prior to the Koreans, other immigrant merchants filled the low-yield void in the economy, Arabs, Chinese, Jews and others, depending on the historical period.

Lack of economic resources from within minority communities drew in immigrant groups to fulfill a specific economic role. The role of the Korean merchant is part of the compartmentalizion of immigrants within the economy.

Photo: Siomara Cramer

Asian Grocer in Los Angeles' Central Market

These Koreans entered a narrowly-confined business arena, constrained by the hegemony of corporate chain stores. Koreans and other grocers received the crumbs of the retail economy while ironically preserving the institution of the ma-and-pa store.

The momentary historical phenomenon of the Korean merchant precipitates false stereotypes. It is obvious that every Korean in South Korea is not a merchant, nor is every Korean merchant successful. Furthermore, according to Abelmann and Lie: "the stereotyped image of the Korean-American entrepreneur, which validates the ideal of the American dream, breaks down against the recalcitrant reality of Korean immigrant lives in the United States. Some Korean dreams have turned into American nightmares, oneiric blue into ominous blues."

The diversity of Korean Americans in Los Angeles, even within Koreatown, is considerable; class, income and cultural identity differences contradict the post-riot media stereotypes. Recall the evidence that first-generation immigrants, with their national identity intact, enjoy intangible advantages over subsequent generations. Although 35% of Korean-American adults are self-employed, only 11% of Korean-Americans born in the U.S.A. are self-employed, a lower proportion than their white counterparts.

Also recall that the culture dilemma of second-generation Korean and other Asian youngsters has led to a plethora of Asian gangs in L.A.

A 1991 fatal shooting of a 15-year-old African-American girl by a Korean-American female grocer exacerbated resentment against Korean business owners, especially after the grocer, convicted of manslaughter, was given probation by a white judge.

"As long as Korean businesses in black neighborhoods hire more Latinos than blacks, they are open to a charge of bias," writes Pyong Gap Min. Only 5% of employees in Korean retail businesses were black and Korean garment factories employed nearly all Latinos.

As Latinos move into South Central Los Angeles (Koreatown is already a Latino neighborhood), Korean-Latino relationships come into prominence. Contrary to media portrayal, the majority of looters of Korean businesses during the L.A. riots were Latinos. Poverty itself rather than ethnic background was a primary cause of the looting. Had the stores been owned by a different ethnic group, they would not have escaped the wrath and anarchy in the wake of the Rodney King verdict.

Avoiding the Culture Quake

Readers who plan to do retail business within the California quilt of ethnic and minority neighborhoods would well follow the path of Koreans who have done it right. Many Korean-Americans have reached out to the African-American or Hispanic neighborhoods where they do business, through food programs, community donations and scholarships.

In New York, Korean merchant Won Duk Kim, a "pioneer bridge-builder with African-American neighbors," urged fellow immigrants to hire blacks and set an example, with an all-black four-man work team in his business.

South Central L.A. experienced a touching moment when, at a joint African-American-Korean church service to mark the anniversary of the riots, a Korean group sang the moving civil rights song, "We Shall Overcome" in Korean.

Abelmann and Lie suggest that in the California scenario, any fruitful sense of community is destined to be multiethnic. European-American suburbanites, African-American inner city nationalists and Korean-American ethnic purists will find that they must build bridges.

Korean-American Richard Choi, co-founder of Radio Korea in Los Angeles, has revolutionized the concept of ethnic radio, reaching outside his own community to host "Listening to African-American Voices," a weekly program devoted to soothing hostilities and building cross-cultural understanding.

Should you wish to establish a service oriented business in California, you will be well served by an imaginative approach to multiethnic participation, through hiring minority employees, participating in community activities, and supporting programs for the disadvantaged.

The Silent Method

Korean immigrants in search of the American dream play the same role as previous waves of immigrants, filling voids in the economy.

The cherished all-American ma-and-pa store was resuscitated, temporarily at least, by first-generation immigrants who hardly spoke English.

In 1995 another Asian immigrant, this one from Japan, was called on to revive a floundering corporate monster known as professional baseball. The 1994 season-ending strike, triggered by the greediness of both wealthy owners and millionaire baseball players, left a sour feeling even amongst the most devoted fans.

As the 1995 season began, the public was staying away from the grandstands in droves. The business of baseball was tottering on the brink of disaster. Wanted: a typical Western hero, a stoic Gary Cooper, riding in to clean up the town.

With local players tainted by the strike, the Los Angeles Dodgers baseball club looked for someone baseball fans did not associate with the ugly labor strife. They found their potential hero abroad, offering two million dollars to the Japanese pitcher Hideo Nomo.

Nomo had led Japanese baseball in wins and strikeouts the previous four years but had injured his shoulder. Only one other Japanese player had ever participated in major league baseball and that was three decades ago. For the Dodger management it was a two million dollar high-risk bet.

After a rough start, it looked as if Nomo was going to have a good season. But professional sports in the United States belong to the celebrity industry; the question remained: how would this new player who could hardly speak English elevate the image of baseball players in general?

U.S. baseball players who had crossed the Pacific had no easy time adjusting to Japanese *Wa*. Wa means sacrificing individualism for team needs. Wa is often lacking in celebrity-oriented baseball, where the more bombastic players tend to make the headlines. Could Nomo bring the needed "wa" to California?

By employing Nomo, the Dodgers were following in their own tradition, having been the first major league team to hire a black player back in the fifties.

Surely, part of Nomo's unusual popularity involved his fine pitching. He was named to start for the National League team in the midseason All-Star game. His "split-fingered fastball" came to home plate "like a gull going for a small fish."

But baseball had many fine pitchers, none of whom attracted such a large legion of fans to the ballparks and souvenir stands. Performance alone did not make Nomo a hero. Nomo's *wa*, the antithesis of individualistic U.S. baseball celebrity culture, was enhanced by a language gap.

Many big-time professional athletes seem so desperate to create a mystique about themselves that they engage in either hyperbole or "trash talking."

"Nomo doesn't talk trash because he doesn't talk at all, at least not in our language," wrote Mike Lupica in *Esquire*. Lupica labeled Nomo "Mr. Nice Guy."

The mystery element, nurtured by his silences, was a primary factor in charming his fans in California.

"Once he learns the language," said Dodger second baseman Delino DeShields, "he'll show everybody who Hideo Nomo really is."

The typical Western hero is a stoic, and the silent Nomo seemed to be as unruffled as they come. When he did speak, it was through an interpreter.

Nomo's manager at the time was Tommy Lasorda, nearly as famous for his Italian-American eating habits as for his baseball managing skills. Lasorda would often serve "the world's greatest Italian deli" for the players after the game.

"Other than Japanese," Lasorda said, "he (Nomo) seems to be most fluent in the international language of food. He may speak Japanese, but the guy sure can eat Italian."

Nomo is universally loved by all Asians, according to one Japanese-Korean-American fan.

Fourteen years before Hideo Nomo put on an L.A. Dodger uniform, a similar saga unfolded around the Mexican pitcher, Fernando Valenzuela. In 1981, Valenzuela, who also spoke through an interpreter, guided his team to a World Series championship.

In the early season, the fans had already fallen in love with Fernando. Songs were written about him, and he filled stadiums every time he pitched. What was once "Fernandomania" is now "Nomomania."

The Nomo story is Part II of an ongoing drama called "The Silent Pitchers." Could it be that Americans have a liking for foreigners who use few words and simply do their job? Or does the silence help create a prototypical character, a stoic who neither brags, nor complains, nor engages in typical sports cliches. Other baseball teams will inevitably import Japanese players.

But as usual, it happened first in California.

DRIVING YOU MAD

"I'm not sure I'll ever adjust to the lack of an easy subway system here," says Karl of Los Angeles. "In London, I could hop on a metro and go anywhere I wished."

Karl had left the east coast of the United States in search of a more pleasure oriented life style. He is delighted to have chosen Southern California, but he did not fully anticipate the culture shock he would experience when his life suddenly depended on an automobile.

"I first moved to Tujunga (San Fernando Valley north of L.A.). My life went from house to car to work and back. This was wrong. The driving time took away from other more human activities. What can you do for hours in the car? Listen to the news, which often does not tell you much?"

Karl's solution? Helped by a precipitous decline in real estate prices, he was able to find a house in a more pedestrian friendly neighborhood. He chose Venice, a counterculture community on the coast of Los Angeles.

Adding to the pedestrian friendliness of Venice are numerous street murals, sidewalk cafes, canals designed by Europhile Abbott Kinney, and the famous boardwalk (cement walk) where street entertainers and misfits find a permanent hangout.

Karl easily adapted to the seductive enclave. The equation of the change of venue balanced a higher housing cost and less living space with a significant reduction in transportation costs since goods, services, and entertainment were all within walking distance. It reminded Karl of his lifestyle back in Europe.

"In other neighborhoods, people spend too much time in their houses and their cars," Karl explains. "It's not natural. Here, we have the cafes on Washington Boulevard. They're within walking distance. I can take a table, read a paper, chat, or engage in people watching."

Driving Etiquette

In most California regions, an automobile is indispensible. Even if you reside in an old neighborhood of San Francisco where places of entertainment and commerce may be reached on foot or by public transportation, a car will get you to the national parks and the seacoast. An awareness of driving etiquette is obligatory. Rules of the road are available in a free and easy-to-read *California Driver Handbook* at any local DMV (Department of Motor Vehicle) office.

The most scenic north/south route is Highway 1, skirting the Pacific Coast, sometimes at sea level, often over high cliffs and winding mountain roads. Farther inland is the attractive highway 101, which passes through Mission towns and vineyard regions. Interstate 5, still farther inland, is the fastest and by far the dullest drive, from the industrial south to a vast agro-industrial emptiness in the Central Valley between L.A. and San Francisco. Parallel to Interstate 5, not far to the east, is the Central Valley's Route 99, a prettier picture of the rich California fruit and vegetable bowl. Route 14 to Route 395 is the eastern-most south/north route, through desert and then rugged mountains and valleys.

Seatbelts are mandatory. Posted speed limits vary. When traffic is not a problem, traffic flows about ten miles per hour above speed limit. Highway limits vary from between 55 to 65 miles per hour. If caught driving under the influence of alcohol or drugs, you may end up in the lockup. MADD (Mothers Against Drunk Drivers) has enormous lobbying influence, and rightfully so. When engaging in social drinking, the accepted custom is to appoint a "Designated Driver," one person in your party who will not drink and will drive the others home.

If stopped by a highway patrolman (you'll see the ominous flashing lights in your rear view mirror), roll down your window and

103

wait for him or her to approach. Arguing with the cop is a bad strategy, and lying that your odometer is broken is even worse. The best "tactic" is the simplest. Be sincere and polite and you may escape with a warning instead of a steep fine.

Visitors to California over 18 years of age may use the driver's license from their home state or country.

For foreigners and New Yorkers alike, the weirdest California traffic law allows pedestrians the right of way, even when they are illegally "jaywalking" (crossing where there is no officially marked crosswalk). At a crosswalk, even with no traffic light, drivers must stop for any and all pedestrians. California's strict pedestrian right-of-way is the last remaining consolation for folks who try to do their business on foot.

"If a pedestrian so much as steps off the curb," writes Arthur St. Antoine, "the entire city is obliged to screech to a halt."

St. Antoine received intensive driver training at racing schools in France, Canada and the United States, after learning to drive in Michigan. For him the culture shock of driving in California motivated the most creative survival methods.

To handle the pedestrian menace, for example, "try bolting a STUDENT DRIVER sign to the roof of your car. It's guaranteed to make them flee from wherever you're heading."

Tailgaiting is probably the greatest California menace, as frustrated drivers squeeze up dangerously close to the car in front of them. For this, St. Antoine developed the GOYA approach ("Get 'em Off Your Ass). His greatest fear: "the guy behind you might be distracted by the sight of a nuclear blonde in spandex hip boots.

"If the person behind you isn't going to stop on his own," St. Antoine suggests that "it's up to you to stop him." The technique requires leaving plenty of room between you and the car ahead. You check the rearview mirror and "if someone is coming up from behind, you brake a little harder than you ordinarily would. That way you force the person following you to slow down on your terms." If it

doesn't work, "you can always ease off your brakes and even touch the gas to scoot safely into the space you've left ahead of yourself."

On freeways, my own cowardly solution is to scoot out of the way of tailgaiters, by changing lanes, even if it requires speeding up to do so. St. Antoine seems anxious to give bad drivers on-the-road therapy. He's been in California long enough to believe that car-to-car communication supersedes in-person contact.

Frustrating commutes have pushed many drivers past the threshhold and too many are now willing to take chances zooming through intersections where the light is already changing to red. St. Antoine suggests that we should treat intersections like cattle crossings, and proceed with the utmost caution, expecting the unexpected.

On two occasions, immediately following motor trips in Mexico, I caught the attention of California road cops by driving in my Mexican mode, too aggressively. Relative to drivers of other cultures, California drivers, who are taught "defensive driving," are still rather polite.

In multicultural California, you will encounter driving style variations you wouldn't find in Kansas. My Mexican friend Javier, whom you'll later meet, insisted that Korean drivers were unpredictably dangerous. Whenever he saw an Asian face in a nearby vehicle, he changed lanes or sped away.

"But Javier," I said, "what about you Mexicans? For you guys, driving is a competitive sport."

"That is true," he said. "But we know what the other guy is going to do. We know he's going to try to beat us to the space when the two lanes become one. With the Koreans, you don't know what they're going to do."

By far the greatest dangers of daily freeway driving emanate from hypnotic boredom or unpredictable fits of anger; anyone can crack after blowing precious hours of one's life in freeway traffic. Therapy comes from the car radio. In most cities and regions, the left side of the FM dial will offer high quality musical or talk programming, commercial free, through affiliates of either National Public Radio or the Pacifica Network.

LIAISONS DANGEREUSES

The automobile culture, the expanding home entertainment industry (VCRs, Cable TV, Internet), computer tie-ins that allow employees to work at home, a paranoid fear of crime, tightened codes against sexual harassment, home shopping, and the general layout of suburban neighborhoods all tend to isolate human beings from each other and their erstwhile community.

The exploding interest in talk radio and internet chats may be a byproduct of the paucity of unstructured human contact. Just glimpse at the abundance of personal ads in free weekly entertainment newspapers, in search of sexual partners (and sometimes plain old friends).

TRAVEL COMPANION WANTED by SWM (single white male), handsome, generous, professional, 6'0", 160. You are 24-35, fit, sweet, lovely, compassionate and compliant. For adventure and fun. Call …

MUSCULAR, GOOD-LOOKING MAN, 29, seeks women, open race and age. Please be serious, reasonable and attractive. Look forward to hearing from you. Call …

ONE VERY SEXY, FUN, CURVACEOUS California blonde, 5'8", 128, 28, seeking very generous benefactor for a no commitment relationship. Call …

It has never been easy to find an ideal partner, but why would these obviously perfect specimens resort to desperate personal ads in their search for true love? Ever since law professor Anita Hill stunned the country with her accusations of sexual harassment against then Supreme Court nominee Clarence Thomas, many government agencies, businesses and schools have created sexual conduct codes; even the most self-assured egotists are now afraid to say "Hey, baby, you're lookin' good" to women at the office or on the street.

In California, the matchmaking business is alive and well. One reputable operation is Debra Winkler's Personal Search. In her first four years in business, Winkler's strictly confidential service has been responsible for more than 500 marriages.

I asked Ms. Winkler why the need for a matchmaking business, and why such success?

"There are no decent places to meet quality people," she said. "You don't expect to find the right person in a singles bar, do you? California in particular is a transient state; people are rarely introduced through family because family members are far off in another part of the country. In particular, California is a car society."

Debra Winkler has served clients whose names would be internationally recognized.

"Being around Hollywood, we've had many well-known clients. You'd think it would be easier for them to meet people, but it's not. Or they may want to avoid people who want something from them. So they come to us."

(Debra Winkler's Personal Search is reached at 310-777-6900 in Beverly Hills.)

Many of the same factors that fuel personal ad and matchmaking businesses make it difficult to develop friendships in general. How does one make acquaintances?

Fitting In

Take Debra Winkler's advice and bypass the singles bar underculture. Look instead for more genuine and spontaneous scenarios for building friendships or finding a mate. The workplace has replaced the community as a breeding ground for friendships. Visitors may not be in a position to work. Increasingly, people are becoming self-employed or working out of their homes. Here are a few alternatives for meeting people with common interests.

- Join a special interest club. Immediately you've bridged the cultural gap. A chess enthusiast from California has more in common with a chess player from Iran than with a soap opera viewer from California. Several newcomers to California have told me of that they were finally able to get involved with other people after joining a club.

- Register for a Continuing Education class. These are non-credit courses in which every student is committed to the subject. If you choose a subject you like, you will automatically be interacting with like-minded people.

- Choose a pedestrian-friendly, mixed-use neighborhood or one that fits with your own cultural persuasions. California has the most varied menu of places in the world. The right place is here, but the odds are against you if you choose a place randomly. (Places with a high level of human interaction are profiled in subsequent chapters.)

- Be a volunteer. California has everything, a plethora of religions, charitable organizations and environmental groups. Pick the issue that moves you the most, and work side by side with others with common goals.

In some places in the world, fitting in involves knowing whether the spoon goes inside or outside the knife, or understanding how close you need to stand in front of the person you are talking to. In free and loose California, surface aspects of etiquette are so varied that the best rule is to simply go with the flow. On the other hand, you may bring your own customs with you, and no one will bat an eyelid. Nigel Sylvester does not feel comfortable with "finger food" and continues to eat hamburgers and pizza with a knife and fork as he did in his native England. No one is disturbed.

(A selected list of organizations and schools with continuing education courses is found in the Interactive Directory at the end of the book.)

FESTIVE CALIFORNIA

The mellow solitude of a brilliant sunset on the California desert can never compare with the loneliness of standing at a parade or meandering through a festival without making any real human contact. California offers a number of impressive, large-scale pageants and fairs where visiters may get lost in the crowd.

Events like the January 1 Tournament of Roses Parade in Pasadena and the sprawling Los Angeles County Fair in Pomona in September are havens for the "Invisible Man" who wishes to remain an anonymous spectator.

These types of events are worthy of visiting and you'll find them outlined in the *California Special Events* calendar, published by the California Department of Tourism, and available as part of a free packet that includes a 115-page Visitors' Guide, a Ski Guide, and maps. You may ask for this free package by calling toll-free: 1-800-862-2543. Foreigners may request the same free package through the mail: California Department of Tourism, State of California, 1201 K Street, Sacramento, CA 95814.

A simple encyclopedic list of each and every one of thousands of California festivals would occupy a lengthy pamphlet and would duplicate the free calendar.

One of this book's objectives is to open doors to new ways of life so that newcomers will maximize their chances for being an active part of the scene. The following annotated insider's list covers a few of the more unusual or participative annual events.

Virtually every festival listed here is FREE.

January

SANTA CRUZ FUNGUS FAIR, second week in January, 70 miles south of San Francisco on Highway 1. Not only will you learn to distinguish between safe and poinsonous mushrooms but guest chefs will provide samples of gourmet mushroom cooking.

Santa Cruz was hit hard by the devastating 1989 earthquake but has managed to preserve its funky ambience, by rebuilding rather than knocking down the damaged structures. Santa Cruz is far less commercial than the boutiquey Carmel and Monterey 40 miles to the south. Redwoods back up against the sea.

Enjoy the oldest beachfront amusement park on the west coast, at the 1906 boardwalk. New-agers and hippies make this town a center for alternative health practices.

Europeans backpackers and bicyclers usually show up at Santa Cruz in the Autumn. Good places for an arriving stranger to sit down and feel comfortable: the Walnut Avenue Cafe or Georgianna's Cafe, both in the garden-like downtown area. (408-425-1234).

February

The **DANA POINT WHALE FESTIVAL** is celebrated at the Dana Point Harbor, in Orange County off Route 1, from the end of February through the first two weeks of March, to coincide with the southward migration of giant gray whales from waters between Alaska and Siberia to the Sea of Cortez, Baja California, Mexico.

The migration is led by females, pregnant cows taking the lead. Courting males are followed by the younger males. Full-grown gray whales can weigh as much as 45 tons (50 feet in length). Bring binoculars to enhance the view.

Whale watching boats charge $14 per adult and $8 for children and seniors, with the skipper narrating the events. Boats depart every hour between 8:00 am and 4:00 pm. On the harbor shore is an ongoing festival with whale-related events. (800-290-DANA)

CHINESE NEW YEAR CELEBRATION, San Francisco, second and third week of February. Best chance anywhere in the U.S.A. to experience China. (415-986-1370)

NATIONAL DATE FESTIVAL, Indio. Mid-February. Includes camel and ostrich races. Best time to be in the desert. (800-811-FAIR)

March

See 26 miles of Los Angeles in an "escorted" tour by running in the **L.A. MARATHON**, on the first Sunday in March. To your possible displeasure you will discover in a most corporeal way that L.A. is a hilly city. For registration information, write to: 11110 W. Ohio Ave, Los Angeles, Ca, or phone 310-444-5544. Fee is anywhere from $50 to $65 depending on how early you register. Fees from abroad must be sent by bank check in dollars, but provisions exist for paying in person prior to the race.

RETURN OF THE SWALLOWS, San Juan Capistrano, mid-March. Swallows have had a long journey, from Argentina. (714-248-2048)

April

The **CHERRY BLOSSOM FESTIVAL** is to Japantown (Nihonmachi) what the Rose Parade is to Pasadena. After enjoying the pageantry, indulge in the Japanese-style communal baths at the Kabuki Hot Spring: (415-922-6000 for reservations.) Services include baths, sauna, steam room, and Amma/Shiatsu massage. A full menu for $65 includes a 55 minute massage, with lower costs for shorter massage periods. Practitioners should be tipped 15 to 20%.

I MADONNARI ITALIAN STREET PAINTING FESTIVAL, by the San Luis Obispo mission, end of April. A great excuse to visit a beautiful little city near the central coast. (805-528-6492)

May

CINCO DE MAYO (Fifth of May) celebrates the 1862 victory of the Mexicans over the invading French army as if California were still part of Mexico. Every region with significant Mexican populations celebrates this holiday. The Spanish words "Cinco de Mayo" are now part of the lexicon of many English-speaking Californians.

If the 26 miles of the L.A. Marathon is too long, consider **BAY TO BREAKERS** in San Francisco, the third Sunday in May, the largest race in the world, according to Guinness. The distance is only 12 kilometers and the race designers have managed to skirt around most of San Francisco's hills, except for Hay Street Hill, on a course that leads from the Bay to the Pacific Ocean. People often run in bizarre costumes. There's a "Centipede Division" in which 13 or more runners are hooked together. Fee is $15 to $20 depending on date of registration.

CARNAVAL, San Francisco Mission District's answer to Mardi Gras, is celebrated on the last weekend in May, with live music, dancing in the streets. A cultural buffet of carnival traditions around the world. (415-826-1401)

Farther north, on Memorial Day weekend, is the **KINETIC SCULP-TURE RACE**, an alternative to the world famous Indianapolis 500 auto race. The event begins in funky Arcata and ends in Ferndale, where a Kinetic Sculpture Museum provides full-time housing for the veteran vehicles. Kinetic sculptures are human-powered works of art. The winner is the vehicle that finishes dead middle of the pack. Two of my favorite winners were an iguana and a banana. (707-822-3619)

Also over the Memorial Day weekend is the **ASIAN AMERICAN JAZZ FESTIVAL** in San Francisco. "Jazz encourages crosscultural interaction," said pianist/composer Jon Jang. "It's so flexible it allows other cultures to contribute to the voice of the music." Coalitions between Asian-Americans and African-Americans in the Bay Area date back to the Free Speech Movement of the 60s at Berkeley. This is the longest ongoing jazz festival in San Francisco.

OLD PASADENA SUMMERFEST, end of May, includes jazz festival and great street life. (818-797-6803)

MICROBREW AND MUSIC FESTIVAL, Suisun City in the Central Valley. More than 30 microbreweries and home-brewing contests. Also blues, Cajun, reggae and rock 'n roll. (707-421-7744)

OPENING MINDS, San Luis Obispo, some time in May. Features exceptional art work by people with mental disabilities. (805-544-9251)

June

OJAI MUSIC FESTIVAL, first weekend in June. Critic Richard Ginell applauds the "iconoclastic charm" of this modern orchestral music festival. Ojai is fifteen miles inland from the coast between Ventura and Santa Barbara. With mountains cutting off the sea breeze, Ojai becomes a summer furnace. But early June is usually safe.

GRAFFITI NIGHT, Quincy, in the Shasta Cascade region, early June. Back to the fifties with music, hula-hoop and yo-yo contests. (916-283-6272)

GAY FREEDOM DAY, late June in San Francisco (415-974-6900) and its counterpart in West Hollywood, L.A. (213-860-0701) are symbolically important even for straight folks. Many of the same politicians who had engaged in gay bashing during the second half of this century were also proponents of anti-immigrant ideologies. Today's acceptance of gay culture in San Francisco and other parts of California opens a political door for all unconventional and immigrant cultures.

The AIDS epidemic adds a tragic tonality to Gay Freedom Day. The Castro is the downtown of gay and lesbian San Francisco. Another gay district is the Polk Street neighborhood. The East Bay cities of Berkeley and Oakland have significant lesbian populations, as do the towns of Eureka and Santa Cruz. In the Southland, West Hollywood, Universal City, Laguna Beach and San Diego have gay enclaves.

On the eve of San Francisco's Gay Freedom Day Parade is the PINK SATURDAY party on Castro Street.

July

INTERNATIONAL WORM RACES, Clearlake in the North Country. Bring your own worms or rent trained ones. (800-525-3743)

The **U.S. NATIONAL SAND CASTLE COMPETITION** draws more than 200,000 people at the unpretentious beach town of Imperial Beach, just north of the border with Mexico. (619-424-3151)

L.A. INTERNATIONAL, mid-July. Organized by the Santa Monica and Venice Art Dealers Association, this cooperative event includes about 50 solo and group exhibitions: artists from Europe, Asia, and North and South America. Each gallery owner chooses his or her favorite foreign artist and sets up a venue. A gallery-hopping feast.

FESTIVAL OF ARTS AND PAGEANT OF THE MASTERS, Laguna Beach, mid- and late-July. Live models recreate classical and modern works of art. (800-487-3378)

GARLIC FESTIVAL, Gilroy, south of San Fran.. (408-842-6436)

August

SAN JOSE JAZZ FESTIVAL, south of San Francisco, largest free jazz festival in the Western U.S. Straight-ahead, fusion, big band and Latin. (408-7557)

SANTA BARBARA POWWOW, representing 40 Native American tribes, second week in August. Join in. (805-496-6036)

Photo: Imperial Beach Times

Imperial Beach National Sand Castle Building Competition. This winning castle was a fortress against beach front development.

WATTS SUMMER FESTIVAL, the oldest African American festival in Los Angeles. People are reminded each year that this eclectic family event celebrates advancements of the community since the 1965 Watts revolt. Nearby, the impressive Watts Towers, by Italian immigrant Rodia, is a reminder of the mosaic sculptures of Gaudi in Barcelona. Rodia was a self-educated tilesetter who cemented this work of art with old pipes, bed frames, steel rods, and anything else he could get a hold of, adding art-nouveau adornments of shards of glass, mosaic tiles and seashells. Dollar tours available on weekends. Phone (213-569-8181) for art exhibits at the Watts Towers Art Center.

AFRICAN MARKET PLACE AND CULTURAL FAIRE, L.A., last two weeks in August, 40 cultures. Free entertainment. (213-237-1540)

LONGBOARD SURFING CONTEST, Oceanside. A great town, and the oldest of surfing contests. (619-722-1534)

115

September

The bio-regional philosophy of Northern California ecologists engenders Arcata's **ALL-SPECIES PARADE** in its **NORTH COUNTY FAIR**. (Arcata may be the only town in the U.S.A. where Green Party and other environmentalists won all seats on the city council.) Participants may dress as any animal, vegetable or mineral in the region. The best species costume wins an award at the North Coast Environmental Ball following the parade. Mid-September equinox harvest ritual. (707-822-3619)

VALLEY OF THE MOON VINTAGE FESTIVAL, Sonoma, is one of the state's top wine tasting events. Sonoma is only a $4.50 bus ride due north from San Francisco via Golden Gate transit. The festival is celebrated on the last weekend of September. Enchanting Napa Valley wine country has become excessively commercialized, whereas Sonoma Valley vineyards still offer free wine tasting. You're less likely to need a car in Sonoma as a few of its 30 wineries are reachable with a rented bicycle, from Sonoma Valley Cyclery, 20079 Broadway.

Sonoma is Jack London country and its nickname "Valley of the Moon" comes from both a London story and a Native American legend. Various wineries offer educational tours and art exhibits. The wineries come to you during the festival. If you like Jack London, Mexican and U.S. history, well-preserved historical architecture, and an eclectic array of gourmet restaurants within walking distance of a lush green Hispanic plaza, Sonoma is a mellow heaven on the rich earth.

The **SAN DIEGO STREET SCENE** includes live music in what is now called the Gaslamp Quarter. Once a red light district, then a skid row, this district was shunned during the Southern California development binge. Result: instead of look-alike condominiums and ugly shopping malls, many of the quarter's older buildings of character survived. When developers finally got around to considering an overhaul of the district, it was too late. Californians were now hip to preservation, and the Gaslight Quarter Council rescued the neighborhood.

Restored buildings from the late 1800s and early 1900s are the scene of restaurants, art galleries, theatres and clubs, with a few of the old flop houses, porno shops and untrendy family businesses preventing the neighborhood from becoming just another gentrified and themish Old Town. San Diego is not usually friendly to pedestrians, but the Gaslamp District is one great place to hang out and stroll around. (619-557-8487)

SAN FRANCISCO BLUES FESTIVAL. For blues in their natural habitat, visit the honky tonk juke joints in the Mississippi Delta in and around Clarksdale. The next best thing is what *Downbeat* writer Dan Ouellette calls "the longest - continuing annual blues festival in this country." Legendary blues artist John Lee Hooker now resides in the Bay Area. (415-974-6900)

PRECIOUS SUNSET POWWOW, Bass Lake in the High Sierra. There are various Native American powwows in California. This one might have the most authentic setting. (209-855-2705)

Photo: Robert Holmes

Wine country in Napa and Sonoma Valleys is the scene of many animated festivals.

117

October

U.S. GOLD PANNING CHAMPIONSHIPS AND GOLD RUSH DAYS, Coloma in Gold Country, early October, with living history demonstrations. (916-622-3470)

STEELE WINE HARVEST FESTIVAL, Kelseyville, North Country, music and wine tasting plus grape stomp and vineyard run. (800-525-3743)

HALLOWEEN, October 31, is the U.S. equivalent to the Day of the Dead and All Saints Day. Traditionally, children (and adults who remember the child within) go out trick-or-treating. Make yourself a weird or scary costume, then stroll through the neighborhood, knocking on doors. The treat is candy. If the neighbors don't give you a handful of sweet things, you're supposed to play a trick on them, although that never happens.

During an episode of paranoia in the eighties, poison was discovered in one child's candy. It turned out that the poison had come from the child's own household. But after TV and tabloid feasts on the story, many folk sincerely believe that it is dangerous to go out on Halloween. For some children, the holiday is ruined as apprehensive parents watch over them too closely. Halloween is probably the most imaginative national festival in the U.S.A.

November

DEATH VALLEY '49ERS ENCAMPMENT, Furnace Creek, mid-November. Desert walks, horseshoe tournament, square dances, cowboy poetry, and gold-panning championships. (619-852-4524)

Pasadena's irreverent **DOO DAH PARADE** is a spoof of the upcoming Tournament of Roses Parade, with float ideas too outlandish to have made it to the January 1 classic.

December

OPEN STUDIOS, Berkeley, October weekends. Self-guided tour of more than 100 artists' studios. Viva Berkeley! (510-845-2612)

TREK TO THE NATION'S CHRISTMAS TREE, Sanger/Kings Canyon National Park, mid-December. The trek ends with a nondenominational service at the base of the General Grant Tree. Between the Central Valley and High Sierra. (209-875-4575)

LAS POSADAS. Many California cities and towns offer Mexican pageants reenacting the journey of Mary and Joseph to Bethlehem, with group singing. (213-628-3562 in L.A.)

In many enclaves of California, from Venice to Santa Cruz, daily life is an ongoing festival. These places are not at all frivolous, nor are they lacking in substance. But gloom is not their nature. One could enjoy this festive California syncopation without attending a single annual fair. The profusion of cafes, night clubs, theatres, free outdoor concerts, and venues of daily street entertainment is mind boggling.

But if festival lovers planned it right, they could begin at the January 1 Rose Parade and move from one festival to another without missing a beat, finishing the year-long binge on New Year's eve. Perhaps a well-financed reader of *Culture Shock! California* will try the idea. Attend continuous California festivals for a whole calendar year and make it into the *Guiness Book of Records*.

There are 188 official ethnic festivals alone, including: African-American, Armenian, Bavarian, Brazilian, Cajun, Caribbean, Celtic, Chinese, Cornish, Danish, French, German, Greek, Hawaiian, Hungarian, Irish, Italian, Japanese, Jewish, Mexican, Native American, Norwegian, Philippine, Polish, Scottish, Spanish, Swedish, Tahitian, and a variety of mixed festivals which involve a number of other ethnic groups.

U.S. CUSTOMS

In *Culture Shock! California*, the "way of life" theme is approached through living examples rather than abstract assertions, emphasizing what is distinct about California. But California is part of the United States and it shares many national persuasions. In the interest of cultural context, a brief outline of pertinent national customs should help foreign visitors to California. American readers who have never stayed in a foreign country may raise an eyebrow when discovering that some of the practices they consider universal appear to foreigners as idiosyncratic to the U.S.A.

The following annotated, alphabetical list contains key cultural categories, based on interviews with foreign observers, but also including a few subjective impressions. Remember, in a diverse California, even the most accurate generalization will have its valid exception.

America

People from the U.S.A. call themselves Americans. The Americas stretch from northern Canada to Patagonia in South America. Argentines are Americans, as are Mexicans and Canadians. Until they adopt the word "United Statesian," we are obligated to use both noun and adjective "American" in reference to the U.S.A. Some Latin Americans accept the linguistic fait accompli, calling us *Americanos* while others coin alternative words: *gringo, yanqui.*

Bargaining

Bargaining is not as inherent to commerce as it would be in Bolivia, Thailand or Tunisia. But surprise! We are learning the art. Expect to bargain for big ticket items (houses and autombles); failure to do so will result in an overpayment. In multicultural California, sales personnel won't judge you as crazy for trying to get a better price. You have nothing to lose by bargaining for a TV or a VCR; the worst they can say is "no."

Bathrooms

After having lived in Europe, we were thrilled with an extra toilet and sink in our home. When it came time to sell, prospective buyers said our house would have been just fine had it contained another bathroom. More bathrooms allow Americans to cultivate their delight in privacy. No wonder they call it "the rest room."

For some Americans, the bathroom doubles as a library, with a table for magazines. (This is no joke.) It's not unusual to find bathrooms with wall-to-wall carpeting.

When we travel to other lands, even those of us who despise fast food chains exclaim: "Bless thee McDonald's for providing a clean bathroom at a time of need."

Bluntness

One man's honesty is another's social clumsiness. Americans tend to be quite direct, and may seem pushy, especially to some Asian visitors. On the other hand, to some Middle Easterners, who stand closer during conversation and speak in longer passages than we do, Americans may appear to lack assertiveness.

"Assertiveness training" is considered a good thing. Paradoxically, we try to avoid certain themes, especially politics. I've seen French people heat up in political exchange but remain friends. For some Americans, a good old-fashioned argument could mean the end of a friendship.

Bribes

In some countries, bribery is an efficient system for getting things done and avoiding the bureaucracy. Why lose a day's work in traffic court when you can pay the highway patrolman on the spot? It is illegal for the "average Joe" in the U.S.A. to engage in bribery. Don't try. Indirect bribery is legal in the realm of political donations, but if you want a policy decision to help your business, you'd better be prepared to make a hefty donation. Hedge your bet by donating to both parties. Because of recent scandals, donations by foreigners are being returned. Yet U.S. foreign policy continues to allow covert donations to influence foreign elections.

The Customer is Always Right

Who cares if they really mean it? It feels good to be greeted by a smile, and even better to be immediately compensated for the slightest mistake of the enterprise. If you're not pleased with the product or it has a defect, take it back with the receipt and you will get a refund. DON'T FORGET TO KEEP RECEIPTS.

Dinner Invitations

What do I wear? Do I take a gift? Do I offer to help in the kitchen? Do I arrive on time or a half hour late? Do I kiss the host or simply shake hands? In California, there is no one dominant etiquette, and this makes it perplexing for the newcomer.

Prior to the event itself, there is a preliminary chat in which the guest may ask the host questions like:

"May I bring a desert?"

"Is this a formal gathering?"

In that conversation, you may be told that it's a "pot luck" which means that each of the guests brings something. In multicultural places like California, hosts of pot lucks appreciate something different, so a dish from your home country is a good bet.

Most decisions of etiquette may be made during the affair after observing what other guests are doing.

In general, dinners tend to be informal, with a wide array of clothing alternatives. A bottle of wine is a standard and appreciated gift, as are flowers. In general, people arrive on time. Unless it is a formal party with hired help, nothing is lost by offering to help in the kitchen. The host may accept your offer or tell you "that won't be necessary, just make yourself comfortable." Shaking hands upon arrival is always proper and in recent years, kissing a host of the opposite sex on the cheek is common. After women have become friends, they may kiss each other on the cheek, but men do not.

Foreigners

> *You may come upon Americans who are incredibly ignorant about your country.*
>
> —Alison Raymond Lanier from *Living in the USA*

In school, we are taught that we live in the best country in the world. Television coverage of the Olympic Games is mostly limited to matches in which American athletes participate. In movies in which Americans are in foreign countries, foreigners are often ridiculed. We grow up learning that foreigners are not as smart as we are.

Many foreign elites become proletarianized in the U.S.A. after hearing stereotypes about their cultures. Americans who have lived or studied abroad tend to discard the stereotypes they were taught.

Friendship

> *It's possible to love a human being if you don't know them too well.*
>
> —Charles Bukowski

In his *American Ways: A Guide for Foreigners in the United States*, the perceptive Gary Athen makes a disturbing observation, based on years of experience as a foreign student advisor. He paraphrases: "Americans just don't know how to be friends," many foreigners say. "You never feel that you are free to call on them at any time, or that they will help you no matter what."

"Americans tend to relate to each other as occupants of roles rather than as whole people," Athen adds.

My wife, from a traditional culture, wondered whether my many horseplayer comrades would remain friends if we were to lose interest in handicapping the races. Can people be just friends, or must they be bowling friends or business friends?

My 17-year-old daughter Siomara comments on the U.S.A. from a perspective of having lived in Mexico.

"If you begin talking to a stranger, they think you want something from them, unless there's a structured reason for talking to them. It's almost shameful. Their self-reliance is important and they don't want to seem too weak or dependent on anyone. Americans have been taught to think that to be successful, you have to compete, and that includes competing with friends."

Siomara reminds us that "these are generalities. It's like saying it's colder on the east coast than the west coast in December. Once in awhile, it's warmer back east than in L.A."

Those predominant ideas, values and behaviors of "Americans" are of the white, middle class, Athen specifies.

One of the exalted values of the suburban middle class is privacy. His comments on friendship seem especially rooted in suburban ideologies. Both companionate marriage and the dominance of the nuclear family tend to wall out same-sex friendships.

On the other hand, in the United States, non-sexual opposite sex friendships are possible, a scenario much less likely in more traditional cultures.

At a typical get-together in Latin America, the men separate to talk about their common interests, as do the women. At a parallel get-together in the United States, the sexes tend to remain mixed.

A twist on the privacy theme is illustrated by the current mania for internet friendships, which allow people who have never seen each other to share intimacies to a startling degree, while still maintaining their distance and privacy. It's sort of what happens in a Mexican bar after every guy is plastered.

My feeling is that, rather than intrinsic cultural values, the physical setting, especially mixed-use zoning and the private automobile, forces people into a privacy mode they may not want. Evidence? A profusion of support groups in which people open up and share their most intimate feelings.

Guns

Why do so many Americans own guns? Conditioning from TV shootouts? A high crime rate? Phallic symbolism? Statistics say an American gun owner is more likely to die by his own gun than stop a criminal with it.

History

> *Americans are generally less concerned about history*
> *and traditions than are people from older societies.*
> —Gary Athen

When Americans declare "that's history," they mean it's all over and no longer of consequence. If you've angered someone enough for him to tell you "you're history," you may not have enough time to look up the phrase in your slang dictionary; it means "you're dead." Preservationists who do care about history may be forced to resort to power politics in order to prevent forward thinking futurist city planners from sending in the wrecking crew to purge the neighborhood of buildings of architectural wonder.

Individualism

We are trained to perceive ourselves as masters of our own individual destiny. Close-knit communities, extended families and other collective entities are of secondary importance compared to our ability to "go it alone." We are expected to leave our parents' home as early as college age, or by the age of 21 if we have not attended a university. Both the offspring of senior citizens and seniors themselves may feel uncomfortable about residing in the same home. Americans considered it a national dilemma when young adults were moving back in with their parents for economic reasons; support groups sprung up to help parents "cope" with having adult offspring in their homes.

Ever since childhood, many of our heroes of popular culture are "loners," as epitomized by the Lone Ranger, Superman, and Rambo.

125

We ignore collective heroes from our own history; most Americans will not be able to tell you anything about those who fought for the 40-hour work week, even though the Martyrs of Chicago are well-known in other countries.

In professional sports, individual statistics are emphasized over team spirit.

It is ironic that cult worship of self-reliant individualists has numbed our own individuality; many of us delight more in vicarious TV contact with a celebrity than in a cup of coffee with our neighbor.

The ideal of privacy has been written into an array of laws, and American individualism goes hand in hand with dogmas on private property.

California is the scene of a number of challenges against the extremes of privacy. We have seen how John McKinney trespassed on private property to make his point in favor of public coastal access.

Junk Food

When we lived in Europe and South America, what did our son miss the most from the U.S.A.? Junk food. Other American parents who have lived abroad tell the same story.

Litigation Industry

In most countries, if you slip in a theatre as a result of someone's spilled soft drink, it is not considered the fault of the theatre owner. But in the U.S.A., the injured party can sue the theatre.

A whole litigation industry, involving lawyers and doctors, may converge on you should someone injure himself on an uneven sidewalk in front of your house.

Disagreements that in traditional cultures are resolved between contending parties are left in the hands of lawyers.

Everyone agrees that people and institutions must be held responsible for true fault or negligence, but most Americans believe that litigation has gotten out of hand.

Niches

> *Californians invented the concept of life-style. This alone*
> *warrants their doom.*
>
> —Don Delillo

Did niches exist before marketing campaigns or have the marketeers increasingly compartmentalized us into niches? Englishman Nigel Sylvester has observed that young people here show little interest in engaging in conversation with their elders. Besides age niches, there are sex niches, lifestyle niches, generational niches, social class niches and educational niches. TV programs are created in order to sell niche products. The niche has replaced the community.

In Latin America and Europe I have attended parties at which three different generations are able to have a good time in each other's presence. This is not to say that niches do not exist in these traditional countries, but they are less pronounced than in the U.S.A., where a cross-generational party, for example, is a rarity.

There is much disagreement as to the extent of the cultural impact of the corporate media. Niche TV programming has had at least some impact in compartmentalizing the culture and limiting social options.

Numbers

If you want to fool an American, give him numerical proof. Multiple-choice tests still dominate many sectors of the education establishment, because Americans often equate numerical results with objectivity. Never mind that the choice of questions for the multiple-choice test is subjective. Some minority groups have protested that such tests exemplify cultural discrimination.

Horse race handicappers bet with blind confidence on "speed figures" because they are quantifiable, and reject non-numerical analysis of the class of the horse that may produce surprising results at a bigger payoff.

American professional sports broadcasts include a profusion of statistics, some of them meaningful, and others absurd. Bolivians were surprised to learn that their star soccer player Etcheverry led the U.S. Soccer League in "assists," because they had never kept stats on passes that turned into goals. Enormous sports data bases churn out meaningless stats: "Wade Boggs is hitting .360 (36%) with runners on third base."

Politics

> In America you can go on the air and kid the politicians,
> and the politicians can go on the air and kid the people.
> —Groucho Marx, comedian

> It makes no difference who you vote for – the two parties are
> really one party representing four percent of the people.
> —Gore Vidal, novelist

Many interviews with foreign students and politically active folks in Europe and Latin America uncover a perception that we Americans are naive politically. In the U.S.A., political discourse takes place in a very narrow frame within the ideological spectrum. The days are numbered for politicians who stray too far afield. For making statements that would be quite appropriate within the European or Latin American political arenas, Californian Jerry Brown was labeled "Governor Moonbeam." The California political scene is relatively more amenable to alternative views, particularly at the municipal level.

Privacy

See **Bathrooms**, **Friendship** and **Individualism**.

Safety

Many Americans first learn of their own extreme safety conscious-ness when they step into an open manhole in other less cautious countries. Nowhere else in the world is the insurance industry, which essentially sells people wagers against themselves, so powerful. (You "win" if you die early or have an automobile accident.) Is this common sense or paranoia? If you've ever inhaled the thick blue smoke in a French cafe, you may agree that it is common sense to ban smoking in restaurants. One extremely bright woman I know purchased a state-of-the-art safety seat for her infant and then sped off with the child at 75 miles per hour. Go figure.

Many families move to a boring suburb to escape the urban crime scene and then purchase elaborate burglar alarm systems and won't let their kids walk home from school alone.

Where is it safer to live, in the city, where crime is more prevalent, or in the suburbs? Referring to statistics in *The Car and the City*, by Alan Durning, "while suburbanites less often fall prey to criminals, they are much more likely to be killed or injured in a car crash. The net result is that suburbanites are actually at greater risk of life and limb on a daily basis than city residents. Durning's stats are based on census, police, and Justice Department data.

Social Class

In his October 16, 1995 *New Yorker* article, "Who Killed the Middle Class," John Cassidy, armed with census bureau statistics, calculates that "living standards have fallen or stagnated for the majority of Americans, while a small minority have enjoyed a bonanza.

He asserts that the term "middle class" has lost its meaning and that the U.S.A. is "a society of diverse economic groups suspicious of both the future and each other." Recent votes in California against affirmative action programs may reflect such suspicions.

According to the Federal Reserve, "1% of U.S. households controlled 38% of the nation's assets as of 1992."

Taiwanese immigrants David Sun and John Tu, owners of a highly successful Fountain Valley, California, technology company, decided to go against the trend by awarding their employees $100 million in 1996 Christmas bonuses, an average of $75,000 per employee, as much as three times the annual employee salary.

Can two immigrants restore the American middle class?

Television

> *I must say I find television very educational. The minute*
> *somebody turns it on, I go to the library and read a good*
> *book.*
>
> —Groucho Marx

TV is an icon and California has produced the iconoclast, Jerry Mander, author of *Four Arguments for the Elimination of Television*.

The Society for the Eradication of Television (SET) opposes "electronic lobotomy." SET believes that "television makes you less an autonomous individual and more prone to being dominated." P.O. Box 10491, Oakland, CA 94610 (415-763-8712).

Time

Time is a resource. In conversation, if you don't "get to the point," you are "wasting my time." The quick "sound byte" has definitively replaced eloquent oratory in political forums. Don't feel offended if, in a chance street encounter with an American friend, he says after a brief exchange: "Let me call you; we'll have to get together." In Mexico, these two friends would have dropped their pressing business and gone to the nearest bar. When efficiency is at risk, friendship can wait.

Nowhere is the concept of "using the clock" more apparent than in sports. In soccer (not a popular media sport in the U.S.), there are no time outs except for injury, but in American football, the "time out" has become a major element of strategy.

Interest in Zen and meditation among many Californians is in direct cultural contrast to the dominant view of time.

Don't forget: arrive ON TIME for business meetings.

Written Word

The Internet, Cable TV and other modern wonders may be altering the cultural value of writing but thus far, when it comes to credibility, the written word still packs a powerful punch. In traditional countries, people are more likely to do business with a handshake. In the United States, written contracts, even among friends, are considered indispensible.

Zen

Americans expect you to get to the point, and expect that the facts will determine the ultimate truth. Zen masters, who do not search for truth by accumulating facts, would not fit in well in American higher education. But here in California, Zen is alive and well. The most well-known home-grown Zen philosopher was the late Alan Watts, whose witty narrations are heard on tapes broadcast over KPFK-FM radio (L.A.) at midnight.

One could arrive in California with a profound sensitivity for cultural nuances and still find the human landscape confusing. An awareness of the great issues that affect daily life in California is a must for anyone wishing to be able to participate in public discourse. California's major issues will be the theme of the next four chapters.

— Chapter Five —

CULTURE CLASH
CALIFORNIA:
ALIEN INVASION

*The world is full of willing people; some willing to work,
the rest willing to let them.*

—Robert Frost, poet

"We confront a silent invasion: hordes of illegal aliens, most of them from Mexico and Central America, are overrunning California, wrecking our economy, disabling our public school system, wreaking havoc on our criminal justice system, and irreparably altering the face of our culture."

This generic manifesto is trotted out by ambitious politicians in search of a winning issue. The rhetoric is supported by all kinds of statistics: the thousands of jobs that illegal aliens take away from

Americans, the millions of dollars in resources they drain from public assistance budgets. The illegal immigrant population now tops five million in the U.S. with more than two million in California, according to an *L.A. Times* report (February 8, 1997).

It's pretty convincing stuff. The fear is real. Aliens, by Hollywood definition, are ghastly invaders from outer space. Most Californians don't know these undocumented immigrants personally; they are seen from car windows: short men with mustaches, dark skin, dark eyes, straight black hair, hanging out at designated street corners and parking lots, hoping that a benevolent pick-up truck will screech in and cart them off as cheap labor.

In France, extreme-right politician Jean Marie le Pen receives 15% of the vote with similar anti-immigrant rhetoric about Arabs and Africans. In California, Pete Wilson harvested an election victory by cultivating concerns over illegal immigration. It was later discovered that the Wilson household had employed an illegal domestic worker.

Other states also receive waves of undocumented immigrants, especially Illinois and Texas, but only in California does immigration eclipse all other issues. Federal and State laws are passed intending to prohibit employers from hiring the undocumented, and limiting social benefits for immigrants.

History shows that such legislation has little effect in curtailing the flow of economic refugees. Beefing up the Border Patrol has minimal impact. Reported deaths from dehydration on the harsh desert north of Calexico hardly deter hopeful arrivals. News item: "Illegal job seekers perish by asphixiation: locked in trailers of smugglers in human flesh." But newcomers still arrive, some willing to pay the *coyotes* a steep fee, usually between $500 and $1,000 per head.

Why would people risk their lives for low-paying jobs that no one else wants? Perhaps we can find the answers through personal profiles of a few of these intrepid individuals.

FOUR CASE STUDIES

Graciela

Division 20, Superior Court building, Hill Street Los Angeles: Landlords attempt to win court orders to evict tenants. My freelance job was to interpret for Spanish speaking tenants and landlords. Occasionally I'd be hired by attorneys; more frequently, with the approval of the presiding judge, I would translate for tenants who could not afford an attorney. Occasionally, the presiding judge would order me to do a case pro bono for an indigent respondent.

The marshall in charge of keeping order would refer me to those arrivals who needed an interpreter. One morning, he introduced me to Graciela, an olive-complexioned Salvadoran woman with frizzy hair who worked as a maid in homes where they would accept the company of her year-old toddler.

Graciela's name was called. She stood up and responded *presente*. The judge ordered her case sent to Division 3. From my daily experience, I knew that the Division 3 judge nearly always ruled against the tenant. I whispered past her cheap earrings that she should go up to the bench to sign in, but first ask for a different judge. "Different judge," I had her repeat.

She went up to the bench and communicated with the clerk.

"Your Honor," enunciated the attorney for the landlord. "The interpreter is practising law without a license. Ms. Martinez had no way of knowing she could ask for a new judge."

I doubted I'd broken any law with my simple suggestion, but the attorney who accused me was a courtroom regular and enjoyed considerable influence. He was accustomed to winning cases against unrepresented tenants. With his accusation, my heart throbbed with fear.

"Counsel," the judge responded. "The interpreter is helping the flow of our calendar. You leave him alone. I'll send Ms. Martinez to Division 12."

Prior to her trial, Graciela explained her version of the case. The landlord, she feared, was trying to evict her because she had refused his advances. He would rent to women without papers, and then let them know in veiled terms that he would call the *Migra* on them if they didn't make him happy.

None of this would be heard in court because Graciela refused to broadcast her illegal status.

She came armed with other evidence: photographs of exposed electrical circuits, hospital bills proving that her son had been burnt after having stuck his hand into the hole in the wall and touched the exposed wires. Photographs of the sole bathroom in the building serving four units, with dishes piled up in the sink. Her unit had no kitchen. Cooking was done with a portable stove.

Tenants alleging habitability violations were supposed to put the unpaid protest rent in escrow, indicating to the court that they were ready to pay as soon as the building code violations were resolved. Graciela was not aware of these procedures and was late with the rent because of her son's hospital bills.

Judges had the authority to excuse tenants from unpaid rents, if landlord violations were extreme. (In one of the more creative rulings, a judge sentenced a major L.A. slumlord to live in his own cockroach infested building.)

Graciela began with a few impressionistic statements. The judge instructed me to tell her to stick with the evidence. Graciela's evidence spoke for itself. The landlord's attorney was disarmed by her photographs. He seemed exasperated that his client had not been frank with him about the apartment conditions.

The angry judge ordered the landlord to fix up his building and report back to him in a month with proof that the work had been done. Graciela would be excused from all back and future rents until each detail in the order had been fixed.

After the trial, I asked her if she thought she was taking work away from legal Americans.

"Black women, they won't work for less than minimum wage," she said. "The women who hire me won't pay more. I work very hard."

She had no complaints. She just wanted the work. A war was raging in her country and death squads ran rampant.

She had lost a day's pay because of her court date. I gave her my phone number, telling her she could pay for my interpreting when she felt she had enough money. She still owed the hospital.

She called a week later, but I was not home. My wife took the message. Graciela's call seemed like an act of good faith. She had no phone of her own. We left for a vacation and never heard from her again.

Javier and Gregorio

During one summer, I took off from my teaching responsibilities to work at a picture frame factory at an industrial park in Culver City. I could have gotten a better job (my salary in the factory was a dollar above minimum) but the location (within a mile of my apartment) and the opportunity to get first-hand knowledge of the working conditions of illegal immigrants were two convincing incentives.

Gregorio's name fit him well. He was gregarious, with thick, dark eyebrows, deep-set eyes, and a perpetual smile. His warm personality along with his unusual height for a Guatemalan (about 6'2") helped catapult him to unofficial leader of the contingent of about twenty undocumented employees.

Javier, Gregorio's elder by about five years, walked me through the different factory procedures with the patience of a Buddhist master. After me, he was the only other employee allowed to escape the summer inferno and make deliveries of tacky framed paintings to interior decorating companies in the L.A. basin.

Javier had a professional degree in his native Mexico, but had found the entry-level salaries to be far below subsistence level. His goal was to work hard, two shifts if necessary, and save up enough money to start his own business in Mexico.

On one occasion, I was in the uncomfortable position of needing to phone the Department of Immigration and Naturalization to find information about a student visa for a neighbor. I was obligated to make the call from the factory, because Immigration only answered phones during work hours.

The factory phone hung in an open area just inside the exit door, where workers would congregate for their ten-minute morning and afternoon coffee breaks and forty-five minute lunch period. I attempted to make my call at 12:30, when my companions would have finished their sandwiches and be outside in the parking lot kicking around a soccer ball. But the dreary rest area, with its old crates as seats and its dusty cement floor, was always occupied by at least one or two employees. For two workdays, I spared myself the potential misunderstanding by putting off the call.

The next morning I told Gregorio that I had to call Immigration on behalf of a student, that I didn't want the other employees to think I was calling about them. No problem, he said. He'd explain to our companions.

He never bothered to inform them. During the morning break, I dialed Immigration. Gregorio called out to the other employees seated on crates near the phone:

"Hey, Marcos is calling *La Migra!*"

He tried to sound alarmed, but was grinning from ear to ear. Everyone burst out laughing. They should have been cynics and dealt with me with guarded suspicion. But instead, they trusted me.

Civil war also raged in Guatemala. Gregorio said that the guerillas were fighting a losing battle and wasting good lives. His older brother had become one of those wasted lives, gunned down by a death squad right in front of the family residence.

Gregorio wanted nothing to do with politics. His family had urged him to leave the country.

Javier and Gregorio were the elder statesmen of the factory. They decided to organize an English class and asked me if I'd volunteer to

137

teach. I agreed. But we would need the management to lend us a corner of the factory for an hour after work. With workers living in different neighborhoods, it would be impossible to find another common time and place.

To approach the management with a proposal for the English classes, the best strategy would have been to show them I was a trained language teacher. But to get the job, I had omitted my degrees from the application.

My proposal was simple. I suggested to the co-owner, that it would be a profitable industrial relations strategy to allow the workers free English classes on the premises. It wouldn't cost him a cent, I added.

"They don't really want to learn English," he said. "They watch the Spanish TV station and they stick around with Spanish-speaking people. You're wasting your time."

"It wasn't my idea, sir," I said. "They asked me."

"Believe me, they're not really interested. Forget it."

He may have sincerely believed what he said. Or he may have been rationalizing a deeply rooted interest in keeping his employees disenfranchised so they would be less likely to walk out on him.

The next afternoon, it was over 100°F in the second-floor warehouse where I was condemned for the day. The windows wouldn't open. Had this been a normal factory situation, the employees could have protested about the heat. But given their illegal status, any type of collective bargaining was out of the question. I envisioned a César Chávez arriving to organize the factory.

Chávez himself had faced the impossible dilemma. During the peak years of his United Farmworkers, growers were importing illegal immigrants in order to break the union. Chávez and his cohorts were espousing a grass roots type of cultural nationalism, with traditional Mexican songs like *De Colores* as their emotional hymns; Latin American illegal immigrants should have fit naturally within his movement.

But economic refugees without papers from south of the border knew nothing of a farmworkers' movement, and were desperate for work. They became strikebreakers. Their presence depressed wages. The Mexican majority of the UFW found itself uncomfortably pitted against its own countrymen. The Union never resolved its mixed feelings over the issue.

I lost track of Gregorio after leaving the factory. Javier eventually returned to Mexico, fulfilling a mathematical formula that made his type of migrant work beneficial to the U.S. economy. In his childhood and youth, when he was an economic burden to the State, he remained in Mexico. During part of his productive years, when he was an economic asset to the State, he was in California. When he eventually reached retirement age and represented a potential economic burden to the state, he would be back in Mexico.

Santos

My next-door neighbor, Santos, came from an overpopulated rural area of El Salvador. He would bring a dreary array of documents for me to translate. Even an illegal immigrant could not escape the bureaucracy! I told him that most government documents in California were available in Spanish. But he could neither read nor write in any language, so it hardly mattered.

When tax time rolled around for Santos, I suggested the Long Form, which would make him eligible for tax refunds; his tax prepayments had been deducted directly out of the paychecks. Santos asked for the Short Form instead. He would forego a potential refund to avoid raising a red flag about his illegal status. People like Santos were a bonus for the I.R.S.

Many of Santos' cohorts would drive without insurance. Back home, an accident dispute would be negotiated directly between the two parties involved. Santos himself had purchased insurance in good faith but had gotten confused about the payment schedule; his accident had occurred precisely at a moment when he had missed a payment and was not covered.

139

That he actually was able to obtain a driver's license is a tribute to ethnic solidarity. Unable to read or write beyond the rudimentary, Santos still passed the written drivers' exam, a multiple-choice affair, thanks to information from his Salvadoran buddies.

Santos was big and chubby, with a round face, curly hair and Elvis-style sideburns. He had a wife and a small boy. The boy would slip out of their open front door and toddle across the street unattended. Back home on the ranch, it was customary to leave kids roaming around.

Santos worked two shifts in the kitchens of two different fast-food restaurants. His wife worked as a cleaning lady, with neither time nor motivation to take care of her overburdened rental house.

Santos' friends would drive up in loud, gas guzzling cars resuscitated from junk heaps. They would hang out in front of the house, drinking beer. If Santos had taken away a kitchen job from an American worker, he had returned the favor by providing another job on a beer factory assembly line. As more Budweisers were downed, the echo of Salvadoran voices would skip loudly through the neighborhood. I would go out and tell them to keep their voices down.

They were used to outdoor, rural communities where you gathered at night. That custom was out of place, to say the least, in suburban America. Santos attempted to hush his *paisanos*.

His home was functioning as an informal safehouse for incoming immigrants, but Santos was hardly the ideal candidate for guru when it came to adjusting to the customs of *El Norte*.

With the stream of guests, the conditions inside his house deteriorated. Ultimately, after much prodding, Santos was coerced by the shocked landlady to move out, but not after the fire department had scolded her; they had been sent to the house to quell a fire.

I had mixed feelings about Santos and his gang. They were a nuisance at times, and I wasn't pleased with a fire trap connected to my house. But I knew one thing that the rest of the neighbors did not understand. Santos and most of his house guests were quite harmless as human beings. They just couldn't cross the long bridge from a great thesis (backwoods third world) to a greater antithesis (post-industrial urban).

I must confess that I was happy to see them go. I was not cut out to be a social worker.

Like many of his cohorts, he was destined to return to his native country within two years of his arrival. It was easy to find work in the U.S. but much harder to save money. Back home he would tell his friends how tough it was. But they would hear that he made five bucks an hour when they were making five a day, and the dream would be passed on to another pioneer.

Marcelo

Marcelo, nineteen-years-old, comes from a close-knit family in the state of Guerrero in Mexico. Against the best wishes of his parents, but with their blessings, he set out for California, crossing the Mexican border on foot, through the beaches at the Tijuana border. His goal: to learn English, an asset in Mexico's job market. Along the way, he wanted to make a few extra dollars to help his family.

Marcelo, a secondary school graduate, was a great contrast with rural immigrants like Santos, with little formal education.

Outgoing and eager to learn, Marcelo was put up in the house of a friend, Rolando. Marcelo found an afternoon job selling newspaper subscriptions, and took advantage of free night classes in English at a local high school. He never missed the chance to practice his English with anyone who would listen: a cashier at the supermarket, a bus passenger sitting next to him, a neighbor walking the dog. Marcelo's ingenuous smile caused normally suspicious people to shed their social inhibitions.

He earned enough to pay a symbolic sum for his room and board. He sent most of the rest home to Mexico. He would go over his English homework, asking Rolando's parents for help only after he had tried earnestly to answer the questions on his own.

One day, Marcelo's friend Rolando needed to travel to Mexico to resolve an emergency and asked Marcelo to accompany him. Marcelo could have used a few more months to iron out the wrinkles in his English, but given his solidarity with Rolando, remaining in California was out of the question. He quit the newspaper job, said good-bye to his English teacher and returned to Mexico.

Considering his objectives, Marcelo's stay had been a success. In his half year, he had acquired enough practical English skills to assist him in Mexico's fragile job market, and had managed to send money home to his family.

Politicians often allege that the money sent by illegal immigrants to their families abroad is a drain on the economy. A temporary measure by the Clinton administration to prohibit Cuban refugees from wiring money to their families in Cuba was intended to fuel discontent against the Castro regime.

If Mexico, a friendly ally, were viewed by the same foreign policy standards, then the money sent south of the border by people like Marcelo would seemingly function as a safety valve against social discontent.

Does the outflow of money from illegal immigrants like Marcelo have an adverse effect on the U.S. economy? To find out, researchers would need to employ a complex statistical methodology that takes into consideration the strategic need of U.S. trade interests for a stable political situation in Mexico.

On a personal level, the Marcelos who risk their lives crossing the border and then deny themselves many basic pleasures in order to send money back home are seen as heroes by their families.

THE AMERICAN WORK ETHIC

Pleasure-loving California offers an alternative to the work ethic of the original thirteen colonies.

Illegal immigrants import a work ethic to California. They toil for two shifts if necessary, are frugal, and try to save money. In California, where the play ethic is dominant, the American work ethic's greatest proponents may be the illegal immigrants.

Do they take jobs away from citizens? Or do they fill an employment void by taking jobs too demeaning for the "average" American?

Do they drain the economy? Or do they help the economy by drinking lots of beer, paying for tickets to soccer games, buying cars, and holding down food prices through their cheap farm labor?

Which has a more negative impact on the economy: the flight of industry abroad in search of cheap labor or the influx of cheap labor from abroad as an incentive to keep industry here?

Does the presence of illegal immigrants depress the average wage of other legal workers?

A 1997 report by the San Francisco based Public Policy Institute of California found that as many as half of all Mexican immigrants return home within two years, and less than one-third stay as long as ten years. The preferred topic of conversation among my undocumented work companions at the picture frame factory began with: "When I return to my country, I want to …"

The report added that those who do remain over the long term tend to be legal immigrants with relatively high education levels and steady jobs, those most likely to stay off the public dole. Only 9.5% of illegal immigrants who were parents had their children in the United States, further diminishing the impact that they would have on social services. The study concluded that illegal immigrants from Mexico were not lured by the unlikely prospect of receiving public assistance benefits.

Ira Mehlman, of the Federation for American Immigration Reform responded to the study.

"Even if most go back, you're talking about a very large number who remain permanently. They are contributing to rising costs and rising anxiety for a lot of people."

Anthropologist Fred Krissman of Washington State University explains that for more than a century, some U.S. industries have actively recruited Mexican labor while the rest of society turned a blind eye. "In 1954 during what was called "Operation Wetback," a million Mexicans were randomly rounded up in the United States and deported," he says. "At the same time we were bringing in 300,000 Mexicans in the Bracero program. We had trains running both ways on public money!"

SURREAL ZIONISM

Illegal immigrants come from every continent. Large contigents of Asians arrive in overcrowded ships after having paid exorbitant fees to their "captains."

But the majority of illegal immigration in the state of California comes from Mexico and Central America. The Chicano concept of nationhood, labeled Aztlán, may be compared to Zionism. California was still part of Mexico 150 years ago, much more recent than the ancient Jewish nation in Palestine. Today massive immigration from south of the border is seen by some alarmed observers as an attempt to reclaim California for Mexico.

By the year 2020, Hispanics will be the majority population in California. "In the Southwest in particular," writes English teacher Dudley Barlow, "non-native English speakers are reaching a critical mass which has weakened the arguments for learning English."

This reality causes anti-immigrant politicians to label the new wave of Latino immigration an "invasion." Graciela, Gregorio, Javier, Santos and Marcelo had no notion that they were part of an army. Their's was an elementary struggle for survival.

Some immigration specialists suggest that a one-sided economic relationship between the U.S.A. and Mexico actually forces some of these desperate people out of their country. They cite examples where small Mexican farmers are edged out of the economy by the inflow of capital intensive agribusiness from the United States.

Photo: Siomara Cramer

By the year 2020, Hispanics will be the majority population in California.

If there is any invasion, it is deep down in the subconscious, a surreal event that plays itself out like Breton's "automatic writing," with no premeditation.

THE BILINGUAL EDUCATION CONTROVERSY

The unintentional "invasion" is greatly resented by certain sectors of the population. "Over one million Hispanic children are beginning their classroom experience in the United States in Spanish rather than English," asserts Jorge Amselle, communications director of the Center for Equal Opportunity. He adds that "bilingual education is working so poorly in California that the State Board of Education is backing off from forcing school districts to use native language instruction."

Bilingual education has been a fixture in American public schools for decades. It was formalized with the 1973 Lau vs. Nichols Supreme Court decision, which guaranteed children the right to equity and access to education, including bilingual.

Arguing against bilingual education in *Forbes Magazine*, Diane Ravitch writes that "the dropout rate for Hispanics is 30%, more than double the rate for blacks and four times the rate for whites." Educator José Cárdenas responds that the opponents of bilingual education "don't let the facts get in the way," affirming that prior to bilingual programs, the dropout rate was 80% among Mexican Americans/Latinos.

Georgia congressman Newt Gingrich once called bilingualism "a danger to society." Teacher Roberto Rodríguez responds that "politicians who continue to equate language with patriotism reveal their complete ignorance of educational issues."

Bilingual educators are the first to admit that their methodologies need tuning. "It's not bilingual education that's failing," says educator Elena Izquierdo. "It's models, expectations, attitudes and practices that begin from a deficient model."

These same educators cite successful models. They refer to schools like Dool Elementary School in Calexico, California, as proof that well-conceived education systems can be extraordinarily successful.

Vivian Gutierrez's bilingual classroom: "The problem is not the bilingual, it's the education. Reducing class size is more effective than purchasing computers and fancy equipment. The children need more personal attention."

At Dool, which serves a less than affluent population, students score as well as their counterparts from the wealthy community of La Jolla, California, renowned for its strict academic program.

Betty Goldstein, an experienced middle shool teacher, assured me that Hispanic students coming from bilingual programs generally perform more successfully in her all-English classes than those comparable Hispanic students who came from sink-or-swim all-English classes in elementary school.

Foreigners who come to California with children will want to consider the educational options available. In general, the type of "transitional bilingual programs" approved by law are geared for students who need to bolster their cultural self-esteem and are the most vulnerable in a sink-or-swim classroom.

When living in France, we sent our son to an all-French public school. As an American, he was an "exotic minority" and would not be subjected to subtle or overt racism. Had our son's self-esteem been low or had there existed anti-American sentiments in the school, we would have seen the need for a bilingual program.

If You Are Coming to California with Children

Certain public schools offer second-language immersion programs. Parents considering living in California should find out where these schools are by communicating with the local board of education.

TIP: With the neighborhood school system in effect, arriving parents should first choose the school and then seek housing in the neighborhood served by that school. The quality of schools varies greatly from one neighborhood to another.

If English was Good Enough for Jesus Christ …

Back in 1924, a former governor of Texas, Miriam Fergusen, opposed legislation that would have required every high school student to learn a foreign language. Holding up the Bible, Fergusen declared: "If English was good enough for Jesus Christ, it ought to be good enough for the children of Texas."

Today's opponents to bilingualism are much more sophisticated than Governor Fergusen. They blame the National Association of Bilingual Educators for disarming children of their best weapon of advancement: a thorough knowledge of English. Bilingualists reply that their programs are precisely designed to assure successful transition into English.

Some Americans fear that the presence of alien languages is disrupting their traditions. Their opposition to bilingual programs is grounded in this fear.

Dudley Barlow tells the story of "a bar owner in the state of Washington who refused to serve two Mexican patrons because they did not speak English. On the wall of the bar was a sign that said something like: 'If you don't speak English, adios, amigo."

"I believe her name was Orlander," adds Barlow. "Something tells me that her first ancestors to reach American soil didn't speak English, either. Someone must have served them."

Barlow believes that in many areas of the United States, the "melting pot" is more like a salad bowl, mixing diverse cultures. His solution: "We need to take a cue from business here. The instructions telling me how to set up my computer came in English and Spanish, and the instructions in a box of film or cough syrup come in several languages."

This he calls progress. Whether one agrees or disagrees in theory with English-only lobbyists, historical reality dictates that California is destined to be a cultural salad bowl.

Chapter Six

COUNTERCURRENTS:
WATER CULTURES CLASH

Whiskey is for drinking; water is for fighting over.
—Mark Twain

California's immigration predicament is rooted in the fundamental human need to work, to be productive, and to support one's family.

Another basic human need, water, is the focus of a more intrinsic culture confrontation, this time pitting Californians against Californians. Two opposite world views are at stake.

The first view, the one that has dominated California history since the Gold Rush (mid-nineteenth-century), is the glorification of human domination over nature. Human beings create a better way of life by remodeling their environment to fit their escalating material needs.

The opposite world view assumes that human beings are an integral part of nature and should live in harmony with their natural surroundings. Any system that generates an artificial acceleration of material needs, according to this world view, will disrupt the environment that sustains it.

Of the many plots and subplots of the California water wars, we shall focus on the most representative story, beginning a few years after the turn of the century when the self-trained engineer, William Mulholland, was appointed to build an ambitious aqueduct system that would bring water 330 miles south, from east of the Sierra to the metropolis-to-be Los Angeles.

Sierra runoff, tapped originally from the Owens River and later from streams feeding Mono Lake would become the city's greatest water source. Prior to the remarkable engineering feat, Los Angeles had a meager 100,000 inhabitants compared to San Francisco's 350,000.

Only five years after the project began, a joyous throng of 30,000 people celebrated the work's completion, on November 5, 1913. Civic engineers marveled at the massive inverted siphons, the hydraulic sluicing and other accomplishments.

When the water gates were opened, Owens river water poured through the aqueduct and arrived at Sylmar, gateway to the San Fernando Valley. "The Valley," once virtually uninhabited, became fertile farmland, and later a sprawling suburb of Los Angeles. Frank Zappa's "Valley Girls," hanging out at shopping malls, are direct descendants of the "Mall-holland" project.

Soon after the 1913 celebrations died down, rumors surfaced that Mulholland was associated with business syndicates that had "cleaned up" by purchasing cheap acreage in The Valley.

MONO LAKE

> *Man is a complex being: he makes deserts bloom – and lakes die.*

> —Gil Stern

For years, I lived in "The Valley," flushing my toilet and watering my lawn, helping to dry up the Owens Valley and lower the level of Mono Lake. Driving back from a vacation from alpine Lake Tahoe on the way to Yosemite Park, we stopped at a town at the edge of the Sierra called Lee Vining. Everywhere in the small town, in restaurants, at

151

our motel, on walls, were posters and leaflets calling for saving Lake Mono. At the visitors center, I asked the attendants what it was all about.

For the first time, I had heard the other world view, the one that flew in the face of Mulholland and the Valley speculators. We Los Angelinos were living in a mode of unbridled materialism, much of which depended on the consumption of massive amounts of water. The level of Mono Lake, at the edge of town, had dropped 40 feet since the 1940s.

Mono Lake had no outlet. Its two primary feeder streams, Rush Creek and Lee Vining Creek, had been diverted to serve the Los Angeles basin via Mulholland's aqueducts, after the City of Los Angeles Department of Water and Power (DWP) had purchased a large part of the Mono Lake area in 1941.

Although Mono Lake is too salty for fish, its alkali flies and brine shrimp served as food for four species of birds: the floating eared grebe, two species of phalaropes, and the California gull, which breeds on the lake's islands. As the lake descended and salinity doubled, the brine flies and shrimp that served as bird feed were threatened. The lake also decreased in surface area by 22 square miles, and the islands where the gulls mated were now part of the mainland. Without their island refuge, the gulls had become prey for coyotes.

With 17,000 acres of lake bed exposed, the resulting dust storms created a health hazard.

Aesthetically, the local inhabitants had been robbed of some of the lake's eerie beauty. Mono Lake is the only site in the world where natural sculptures called the "tufa" are formed by the combination of calcium-laden springs bubbling up through alkaline water.

Meanwhile, south of Mono Lake, Owens Valley had been ceding its water to Los Angeles since 1913. With the loss of ground water, this once fertile valley had been severely damaged. In 1970, the DWP opened a second aqueduct and significantly increased its pumping of ground water from the Owens Valley. Agriculture, fishing and aesthetic beauty were all victims.

Tufa formations on eerie Lake Mono – like an Yves Tanguy painting.

Opposing Currents

Supported by various environmental groups, both Inyo County, in the Owens Valley and the Mono Lake Committee have been battling to win hearts and minds, and working through the courts to save their habitat. At issue was a fundamental difference in cultural perspective.

The Los Angeles Department of Water and Power had purchased the land that held the vital sources of water in both Owens Valley and Mono Lake. Since the Gold Rush, Californians have been raised on the concept that "if it's mine, I can do whatever I want with it," including the extraction and transport of water.

A farm in the state of Michoacán in Mexico was the scene of my first exposure to a differing philosophy, one that tempered the supremacy of private property. I would observe a constant parade of local residents, mainly of indigenous background, pass through the private farm (trespassing, I thought at the time), in order to stock themselves with water from two natural springs.

153

COUNTERCURRENTS: WATER CULTURES CLASH

I asked the farm owner about the daily visitors. He cited an unwritten agreement: private property did not include water rights and everyone within the community in need of water was permitted to enter his property and take out what they needed. This custom, as it was practiced in Michoacán, dates back to both pre-Hispanic times in the Americas and to medieval Europe.

My Michoacán experience was echoed in legal arguments by lawyers for both the Mono Lake Committee and Owens Valley. Even if owned by private companies, "certain major bodies of water and the land they lie on belong to the people."

In 1983, momentum in the water conflicts changed sides when the California Supreme Court handed down its "Public Trust Decision." The difference in the vote that favored water rights activists came from three Supreme Court justices appointed by then Governor Jerry Brown. It was a brief window of opportunity for the activists; all three justices were later forced to resign by a more conservative state government following a lengthy campaign against them relating to the separate issue of the death penalty.

Thirteen years after the Public Trust Decision, a transformed Jerry Brown, no longer part of the political apparatus, would applaud "the recognition of general good instead of the nineteenth-century "this-is-mine" premise.

Following the 1983 decision, a protracted water struggle was to be fought in the courts. Allied with the Inyo County suit in defense of Owens Valley, was the Mono Lake Committee, formed in 1979 by David Gaines after his research told him that the lake would dry up within two decades if the DWP continued its water policy.

The Byzantine court proceedings left two world views hanging in the balance. Yet the public hardly noticed. There was no celebrity issue, no Othello-like character that made the O.J. Simpson trial capture the undivided attention of the media. The water issue was just that: only water, something that contemporary consumers took for granted. Only those city dwellers who had visited the lake could relate the image of a lake of unparalleled beauty to the "dry" court proceedings.

Little by little, court rulings in the early and mid-nineties accumulated into a victory for the environmentalists, but not before the Mulholland water project had made Los Angeles the second largest city in the United States and a veritable empire in the industries of defense and cinema.

According to John Hart, author of the authoritative book about the issue, *Storm over Lake Mono*, 125,000 acre feet of water are still diverted from the Mono creeks to L.A. One acre foot is enough to support three families per year, which means that 450,000 families are supported by the Mono creeks alone. Approximately 60% of the L.A. water supply comes from the combined Owens Valley and Mono Lake water sources.

Today, at both Mono Lake and in the Owens Valley, the posters and pamphlets that once urged us to "save" the lake and the valley now call for restoration.

Ruth Galanter, who chaired the L.A. City Council's Natural Resources and Energy Committee said that a 1997 agreement between the city and Owens Valley was evidence that both Los Angeles and its DWP are "committed to doing things with more sensitivity to the environment."

Bob Michener, chairman of the Inyo County Board of Supervisors, believed that the agreement "should go a long way toward having a better feeling between the people who live up here and the city."

The water war has ebbed. But the philosophical contrasts were never brought to the attention of the typical L.A. homeowner, who continues to superimpose the English lawn, a product of the rainy British climate, on the semi-arid Los Angeles basin.

BIOREGIONALISM

The water issue fits within the bioregional movement in California, spearheaded by the Planet Drum Foundation in San Francisco. According to Planet Drum, "a bioregion is a distinct geographic region that has a continuity of watersheds, rivers, landforms, climate, native plants and animals, and other natural characteristics. Bioregions also include cultural values that human residents have developed about living in harmony with these natural systems."

If I understand bioregional philosophy, I said to Peter Berg, founder of Planet Drum, then Los Angeles homeowners should not have neat, watered lawns, not in their dry climate.

Berg confirmed my elementary discovery. And I thought: what would happen if a suburban homeowner, a convert to bioregionalism, decided to help save Mono Lake by ripping out his lawn and cultivating cacti and other rugged plants that would grow naturally in the bioregion? The guy's neighbors would be up in arms. They might run him out of town.

Bioregionalism "puts a modern twist on indigenous people's living strategies." In California, mainly in the north, some communities of Native Americans (the Sinkyone), of hippies (the Matteel), and even whole towns (Arcata) are currently living the philosophy.

"Before 1850," affirmed Berg, "most peoples were bioregional, not colonial/regional. People lived in a valley and called it "our valley." They grew things that grew in their valleys."

Berg asserts that we've made people "dependent on industrially produced resources and commodities. So much of the planet is currently impacted by this one culture that it should be termed global monoculture. It isn't, despite its arrogance, the only culture."

A bioregionalist description of California would differ greatly from our outline of California regions in Chapter Two. Berg, lives in San Francisco but he calls it the Shasta Bioregion on his correspondence because Mt. Shasta is located at the top of the region's major watershed.

"Shasta is a distinct, diverse and interdependent part of the planetary biosphere that deserves a unique social, political, and cultural identity to match its natural endowment," said Berg.

For information about bioregionalism, write to the Planet Drum Foundation, P.O. Box 31251, San Francisco, CA 94131 Shasta Bioregion.

A Larger War

The Central Valley Project (CVP), a complex network of twenty dams and 500 miles of canals serving large agribusiness, is the motive for contentious battles over water. Even after the Central Valley Project Improvement Act of 1992 was enacted in order to balance the needs of agriculture with those of wildlife, wetlands, and commercial and recreational fishing jobs, more than eight of every ten gallons of public water are earmarked for agricultural purposes. The $6.8 billion in water subsidies received by corporate and factory farms may decline with the new measures.

But according to Jim Edmondson, Executive Director of an organization called California Trout, "Victories were won on paper,

157

but thus far there's been a lot of rhetoric and not much action."

The Mono Lake victory was important, says Edmondson, but "eighty-five percent of water in California is not used in the city. That argument was largely between those who wanted water for the environment and those who wanted it for the cities. Agribusiness has done an amazing job in staying out of the water wars."

Edmondson gives us a glimpse of the issue from an historical perspective. There are salmon and steelhead populations from the Oregon border to the Mexican border. During the past 200 years, they have declined towards extinction. The process begins from the south and works its way north.

Following World War II, California's rich Central Valley has been losing these species because of the major Central Valley Project, a network of canals primarily serving large agribusiness.

"We don't have a water shortage in California," says Edmondson. "We're like a bald-headed man with a goatee; pretty good production, terrible distribution. The North Coast is the only place remaining with a semblance of the historic numbers of salmon and steelhead."

Hatcheries have been a dismal failure, an excuse to cover up the damage, Edmondson elaborates.

In the Central Valley there are two river systems, the Sacramento (north to south) and the San Joaquin (south to north).

"In California, water doesn't follow gravity," notes Edmondson. "It flows toward the money. The San Joaquin system runs from irrigation canals directly to agribusiness property.

"You'll see signs that say: 'WHERE WATER FLOWS, FOOD GROWS,' but twenty-five percent of developed water is used to produce only one-tenth of one percent of the state's economy."

Edmondson doesn't blame city dwellers for the water crisis, and praises Los Angeles residents for having made "a major change in behavior." During the drought, water consumption was cut voluntarily by a third, and many people have continued to conserve water in the same ways even after the drought ended. They take five-minute showers, they don't grow things in their yards that belong in the tropics, and they recycle.

Edmondson reminds us that the species on the California State Flag, the grizzly bear, is no longer found in the state. "The state fish," he adds, "the golden trout, is almost extinct too, because of livestock grazing by Anheuser-Busch. It's a question of huge corporate welfare."

THE PRICE OF WATER

"If we price water at its fair market value," concludes Edmondson, "free market principles would solve the problem. Simply remove the massive government subsidies that go to agribusiness.

"From a fish conservationist view, let's look at the cost benefit of leaving water in the rivers. One of the four building blocks of the economy in California is going to be recreation and tourism. Our water is an attraction. People won't come here to fish in dry rivers."

Meanwhile, back at Mono Lake, the target height of 6,377 feet above sea level was surpassed in 1996, when the water level reached 6,380 feet. According to legal agreements, when the lake reaches 6,391 feet above sea level and covers 76 square miles, Los Angeles will be able to divert as much as 30,000 acre-feet of water per year, still considerably less than the 90,000 acre feet it was taking before the 1989 injunction.

Chapter Seven

DEVELOPMENT

From Santa Barbara north of L.A. to San Diego near the Mexican border, the coast of Southern California is lined with view-blocking condominiums, private clubs and exclusive restaurants. The raunchy Venice boardwalk district in Los Angeles and the San Onofre Nuclear Power Plant are amomg the few spots that interrupt this chain of development.

The Venice boardwalk was on the verge of losing its honky-tonk, left-bank ambience when developers proposed to transform the anarchist scene into an outdoor mall. The improvements would have sanitized the boardwalk, effectively phasing out the more grizzly of street entertainers.

But an activist group called Alliance for Survival organized the community against the proposed improvements and the developers ended up with a few conciliatory pavement contracts.

Farther south in San Onofre, with an irony not appreciated by purist ecologists, miles of coastline remain protected from human intervention by a twin-domed nuclear cathedral. An occasional lone surfer takes advantage of the solitude.

THE PORT STOPS HERE

Venice and San Onofre are accompanied by the only entire coastal city of Southern California to engage in prolonged resistence against the mall moguls and condominium magnates: Imperial Beach, known by locals as I.B., the last city before the Mexican border.

Pro-development forces within the city continue to fight for the right to build up the last patch of available coastland.

Through their influence, two Grand Juries, with the power to bring criminal charges, undertook investigations of the Imperial Beach municipal government, whose officials were elected on the basis of their opposition to beachfront development.

"You don't hear much about political affiliations," said Dottie, a long-time resident. I.B. is a one-issue town. The issue is land use."

As the investigations marched forward, the Port District tried to grab off beach area for development. Employing creative tactics, the people resisted. At the U.S. National Sand Castle Competition, which draws 200,000 people annually, the winning castle was an elaborate fortress, with the inscription, "THE PORT STOPS HERE."

With no evidence of any criminal wrongdoing, the Grand Juries wrote final reports attempting to discredit the city leaders. "No commercial structure of any significant size has been built on the undeveloped beaches of Imperial Beach since its incorporation in 1956," one Grand Jury report accused.

What seemed to the Grand Jury like negligence was applauded by the majority of residents as visionary. Developers placed one referendum after another on ballots, which, if approved, would permit beachfront development. I.B. residents rejected each and every one, voting against the easy dollar and in favor of their easy way of life.

Imperial Beach is accustomed to criticism from people who just don't understand. Residents feel harassed by journalists who coin cute nicknames for their unmanicured city, epithets like "Venereal Beach."

The city has earned a dubious reputation for having considered the perils of individual freedom more acceptable than the greater menace of social control. This is the only Southern California city where horseback riding is permitted on the beach. Given the choice between social control and horse poop, the residents chose the horse poop. (Horses may be rented from the D-Bar-D Stables, 619/428-2563.)

Imperial Beach's live-and-let-live philosophy avoids regulations whenever possible, following the precept that "fewer laws make fewer offenders." No license is required to fish for halibut and Florida bass from the T-shaped pier extending 1,200 feet into the ocean.

The human consequences of I.B.'s anti-development/pro-individual freedom position are summed up by Jan Hopkins, co-owner of a tiny seacoast restaurant called My Little Café. "People here feel free to be the way they are, even some who just can't quite get the hang of society."

"Imperial Beach welcomes eccentrics," says John Mahoney, editor of *The Imperial Beach Times*. "It is a comfort to people who don't have very much but don't feel discriminated against or out of place. It has an absence of pretenses."

The type of ma-and-pa businesses and public gathering places that fade away in the shadow of chainstore development in other towns of the U.S.A. are alive and well in Imperial Beach. I.B.'s individuality seems to make newcomers feel most at home.

The Pier Plaza is the focal point for this unceremonious lifestyle, the site of community events and informal gatherings, with a fountain and public restrooms. The International Blends Coffee Shop is one of many local hangouts, where classical and jazz musicians can apply for a Friday night gig by calling 619/429-0340.

Another consequence of the lack of seafront development is the survival of the Tijuana River National Estuarine Research Reserve, one of only 22 in the United States and the best saltwater marsh wetland in Southern California. A free visitors' center offers one-of-a-kind exhibits, including an interactive art genre called Polage, Austine Wood-Camarow's polarized light paintings, seen only through a polarized lens. Colors and figures change as the viewer rotates the polarizing filter.

The political catalyst for the resistance against development defies all labels. One editorial in the *Imperial Beach Times* applauds a city council member's "decision to form a citizens' budget committee, a wonderful step backward, if you will, to a place in the past where it was still common belief that the American idea of self-government was a good one."

Left-leaning anarchists and rightist libertarians seem to find a common ground within I.B.'s hip conservatism.

The fact that the freeway and railroad line both steer west of I.B. means that through traffic between San Diego and the Mexican border never touches the city. In a state where the freeway is the primary channel for commerce and travel, cities only a few miles off the main road become isolated. Even within California, Imperial Beach is a well-kept secret.

A significant Mexican and Asian population lends an international flavor to the city. The high fence that separates the U.S. and Mexico at Imperial Beach does not reach the ocean. One can wade or swim back and forth between the two countries, and jet-skiing lifeguards from I.B. often cross the border to help out on the other side.

Fifteen miles inland, the summer heat becomes unbearable, but Imperial Beach receives the direct flow of the benevolent California current that warms up the winters and cools down the summers. Those undocumented immigrants who have heard the horror stories of desert dehydration attempt to sneak into the U.S. via the surf at I.B. I've met a few who have made it safely by getting lost in the crowds. But most of these economic refugees are caught soon after the crossing.

Imperial Beach is a great place to visit and a better place to settle down. But if you're a dentist or an auto mechanic, there will be more opportune cities in California. I.B. residents can drive across the border and receive dental or automobile repairs for a fraction of their cost in the U.S. My friend Bob reports of a clinic in Tijuana "where a crown, expertly done, is less than $100."

I once took my car to TJ for repairs that U.S. mechanics were reluctant to attempt.

"Oh yes," said Manuel, the mechanic. "I worked in Los Angeles. But there, they are not mechanics. They are part-changers. Here we can revive a dead car."

Imperial Beach is a shy recluse, forced by its geography into a menacing party. On the one side, there are the developers, lusting for the untapped profits of the coastline. On the other, an army of unemployed thirsting for jobs that most U.S. citizens would not dream of taking.

Imperial Beach just happens to be sandwiched between California's two hottest issues: development and immigration. As these two historical dramas play out, I.B. manages to remain its own unpretentious self.

GENTRIFICATION: PASADENA AND VENICE

Civilization is a limitless multiplication of unnecessary necessities.

—Mark Twain

A typical dilemma is faced by places like Imperial Beach and Venice. Bohemians or inconoclast pioneers gain a foothold, add flavor and spice. The developers follow, investors with a vision for manicuring the rough edges and converting local hangouts into yuppie nightclubs, family owned apartment buildings into exclusive condominiums.

A whole neighborhood can be transformed into the consumer modality within a few years, as happened in New York's Soho within Greenwich Village. Well-financed artists bought old warehouses and created a boutiquey neighborhood with trendy outdoor cafes where everyone wears black. In one art gallery, a sign: "MONEY CREATES TASTE."

Parts of Venice have become gentrified, especially around the canals, where a scrawny bungalow rents for well over a thousand dollars a month. Along the boardwalk, some of the offbeat artisans have been replaced by T-shirt vendors.

But Venice remains a contrarian place. Within affluent sectors, many are aware that the boardwalk weirdos, the one-of-a-kind artisans, street entertainers and creative panhandlers give the place a human ecology worth much more than well financed development. A significant contingent of the Venice canal dwellers actually opposes facelifts that might overgentrify the neighborhood.

NEWS BULLETIN: January 22, 1997:
A Wipeout at Venice Beach Graffiti Pit.

Perhaps only in Venice Beach could a whitewash of graffiti be considered a crime. But L.A. police are investigating the mysterious painting over of the image-strewn walls - and benches, tables and trees - in a beachside site known as The Pit. Outraged beach denizens insist that the cover-up is vandalism.

Many Venice insiders fear that gentrification would price out the poorer sectors of the community. The town would risk losing its ethnic and class diversity if it discarded the funky wild card that made it valuable in the first place.

Twenty miles northwest of Los Angeles, Pasadena's historical core was spared the wrecking cranes. For years, it languished in neglect and indifference. From one year to the next, Californians suddenly yearned for more typical townscapes, and Pasadena's smart money began restoring the architectural heritage that other San Gabriel Valley cities, scarred by mini-malls, had lost forever.

The east side of downtown Los Angeles was spared the wrecking crew because developers didn't think it was a good investment. As a result, much great architecture has survived.

I hung out in Pasadena before it was "discovered," before commercial interests began to draw large crowds to "Old Town Pasadena." Today, aesthetically pleasing architecture and quirky restaurants and clubs make Pasadena one of the most alluring places in all of Southern California.

During a period when California real estate values plummeted, Pasadena had become a boom town. Some observers fear that the city is already overgentrified, and will inevitably lose some of its attractive diversity, its homespun character of the past.

WEST BERKELEY

A parallel dilemma was faced by the ragtag array of artists, punk musicians, craftspeople and anarchists who have been occupying old factories and warehouses in the industrial area of West Berkeley, across the bay from San Francisco.

Once the bizarre vanguard of nonconformists had spiced up the neighborhood, developers and commercial interests made their move. If the developers had their way, the original pioneers who made the neighborhood liveable in the first place would be priced out.

An anti-materialist, anarchist spirit brings people to this type of community. Resident Mike Helm says that his neighborhood attracts "people who are trying to live creative lives where they aren't having to work 60 hours a week to pay the rent." The guy who wants to work in a creative pursuit relinquishes the nine-to-five gig, rejects the middle class lifestyle, in exchange for the precious commodity that characterizes the Berkeley flats: personal independence. He gives up the American Dream in order to write the Great American Novel.

Mike once sold his poetry on the street, books like *Snap Thoughts*. He's been the editor of a prestigious publishing company, editor of an environmentalist newsletter, and the manager of an important recycling business called Urban Ore. He now owns City Miner Books, and thanks to the mixed-use zoning in the Berkeley flats, he can operate this publishing business out of his garage.

Mike is the author of several fine books, and he's also published some gems, including Jim Dodge's small press best seller *Fup* that sold 75,000 copies. He plays the horses at nearby Golden Gate Fields, using his personalized breeding studies to make some extra bucks, or hangs out in Berkeley's cafe culture. He rarely crosses the bay to San Francisco because mixed-use Berkeley, nicknamed the "Gourmet Ghetto," has it all.

Mixed-use zoning flies in the face of the prevalent single-use zoning ideology of modern development in the United States. Single-use zoning separates residential and commercial areas. Mike believes

Mixed Use Berkely: Publisher Mike Helm operates his business out of his house.

that a change back to mixed-use would be the most effective way to reduce pollution. If everything is nearby, there is less of a need to drive long distances, or drive a car at all. Within walking distance of Mike's house are several family owned restaurants, a French bilingual school, various industrial structures, and a profusion of small craft cooperatives.

The mixed zoning that Berkeley residents have protected for years is now being rediscovered across the country. David Schwartz, author of *Who Cares: Rediscovering Community*, believes that Ray Oldenburg's "third places" (neighborhood gathering places phased out by single-use zoning) are essential for recreating a caring society.

"If I could take only one government action to increase 'care' in U.S. society, I would agree with Oldenburg that the single most influential thing that could be done would be to eliminate residential zoning that keeps third places out of residential neighborhoods.

The November/December 1996 issue of the conservative *The American Enterprise* features an article that asserts that "Zoning Kills Community Life."

Formerly known as the M-Zone (M stands for "mixed"), the West Berkeley community conceived one of the more creative methods for resisting gentrification. Residents organized, negotiated with developers, and lobbied for local ordinances. The negotiations produced a master plan that institutionalized the mixed-use nature of the neighborhood.

Still, the supply of affordable housing was at risk. The California state legislature then passed a law that superseded West Berkeley ordinances that would have protected the less fortunate from gentrification.

The community responded with yet other alternatives. The clever "Arts and Crafts Ordinance" protects housing space for artists by square footage. If one artist moves out, the space must be rented to another artist. Most artists are not affluent, and the ordinance tends to keep down the cost of rent.

Anton

Originally from New York, Anton Lignell found West Berkeley at about the time he had decided to live a creative life. He rented a cheap room on the property of Spengers, the famous seafood restaurant, and began crafting harpsichords. Eventually discouraged by "the prima donnas who played my harpsichords," he moved to New Mexico and began sculpting rocking horses. Back to Berkeley, he was invited to teach the art of making rocking horses at the University of Berkeley extention program. He did that for five years, producing a do-it-yourself book. One of his rocking horses appeared on the cover of an important woodcraft magazine.

Anton still makes rocking horses, but today's major project is a work of literature called "Last Lizard and the Mathematics of Creation," a humorous fantasy involving Indians, hobos, visions, synchronicity, pool sharks, sailing ships, jazz, polar bears, love, a talking dog, secret letters, a fashion model, and the three principal irrational numbers in the interior and exterior of the Great Pyramid at Giza.

Since childhood, Anton seemed destined to be different. "In school I didn't do homework because I was reading about single-handed sailing around the world."

Anton's products cannot be mass produced and thus do not fit within the corporate economy. He is paid handsomely for what he does, but his market is too small for him to bathe in affluence. West Berkeley is one of the few places in the U.S.A. where a person like Anton can thrive without giving back all his income to rent, auto insurance or a mortgage.

"If the world were a library," says Anton, "then the books that fall through the cracks or behind the shelves are Berkeley. I've sort of become an urban hermit. There are enough strange people around here that I don't feel out of place."

Anton lives in a partitioned area of a former candle factory. The high ceiling allows for a basketball net in the middle of his space.

"I've placed the net at an elevation where I become the equivalent of 6 feet 7 inches in height," says Anton the mathematician.

Berkeley's anarchist artists form a silent resistance that protects their breed from the dissolution that comes with overdevelopment. West Berkeley's blue collar and ethnic minority groups belonged to another at-risk sector of the population. Capital-intensive technology like the biogenetics industry would move in and replace traditional manufacturing, providing mainly professional jobs. To resist the thinning out of its working class sector, West Berkeley prohibited industrial producers from converting more than 25% of their facilities away from manufacturing.

These and other offbeat ordinances allow the community to resist gentrification, remaining mixed in zoning, architecture, cultures, social class. Whites, Latinos, Asians, African Americans and Native Americans are all significant sectors of the Berkeley population.

Anton, Berkely artist in front of his apartment, a converted candle factory. Many Berkely artists live in such factories.

171

"The interaction between the groups is not the ideal we'd like it to be," says Rick, a community organizer. "But at least you see clubs where various groups show up."

Avoiding the predictable path to what Mike Helm calls "the monoculture," this community has developed its own inclusive alternative economy. There are various worker-owned collectives, such as the Ink Works print shop. An organic farm embellishes a formerly empty lot. Salvage operations like Urban Ore allow residents with low finances to live well outside the consumer economy. Trading, bartering and recycling are the underpinnings of this alternative economic culture.

From the shore of West Berkeley you can see across the bay to San Francisco as you fish for a dinner that may or may not be edible. The weather is sometimes too rainy and relatively cool, but there are no extremes to rival the harsh winters and steamy summers back east. Berkeley enjoys pleasant, balmy days year round.

In many other towns and neighborhoods in California, residents are now rethinking the purpose of development and trying to conceive a balance between economic growth and human ecology. Terms like no-growth, controlled growth, mixed use, and bioregionalism now play a significant role in places across California, including Arcata, Berkeley, Hopland, Imperial Beach, the Mattole Valley in the rural north, various districts in San Francisco, Sonoma, and Venice. These places offer a more textured alternative to the modern development formula.

In light of their anti-consumerist tendencies and their opposition to development, these places have been labeled "radical" and "anti-traditionalist" by political conservatives. But Peter Berg, of the Planet Drum Foundation, challenges the prevailing jargon.

"From an ecological perspective, the wild-eyed radicals are the consumers. They are the bikers of the biosphere, who are destroying the basis of life for everyone else on the planet. Those truly interested in conserving things, simple living advocates or those in Earth First, they're the traditionalists."

Chapter Eight

AUTOMOBILE DETERMINISM

L.A.: where there's never weather, and walking is a crime.
—Ian Shoales

L.A. once had a plus 1,000-mile rail system of "Red Cars," known in 1911 as the Pacific Electric Railroad. From the 1930s through 1961, the automobile and oil lobbies convinced the authorities to gut the system in favor of a network of freeways.

Drive-in restaurants, urban freeways and other icons of the automobile culture began in Southern California and spread to the rest of the country. Those who arrive in California from public transportation cities like New York, Chicago, Paris or London sooner or later must deal with the obligation of owning a car and becoming part of a problem that includes pollution, congestion, and an insidious conditioning process that convinces us it's normal to drive fifty miles to have dinner, or to commute to work a hundred miles round trip.

People who were born here believe it is their own decision to drive obscene distances and listen to radio traffic reports every six minutes in which rarely a day goes by without at least one freeway being hopelessly backed up by a fatal accident.

Today, Los Angeles and its Metropolitan Transit Authority are making a belated effort to alter this (free)way of life by building a controversial and costly metro rail system. An operating Blue Line to Long Beach and downtown Red Line subway are part of a projected 400-mile system to be completed in the year 2010.

Meanwhile, the automobile culture dominates the scene. Sooner or later, newcomers to Southern California must decide whether it is better to fight or switch.

TO SWITCH

The first time my wife and I drove from L.A. to San Francisco, we were prepared to use our automobile on a daily basis. After a week's stay, we had only used it once, for a baptismal trip over the Golden Gate Bridge.

Otherwise, we either walked or used the BART (Bay Area Rapid Transit) subways and the MUNI (Municipal Transit Agency) buses. Through a decade in L.A. I had logged over 5,000 freeway hours! And I drove less than most Angelinos.

San Francisco is a walkers' paradise, with real neighborhoods, of distinct character. L.A. has a few real neighborhoods, but one must drive to get to them.

The number one obstacle against well-intentioned walking in the United States is sensory deprivation. On typical streets you feel as if you're on a treadmill. The body wants more exercise but the mind tells it to give up. Much of San Francisco remains the exception: a feast for the senses.

- **THESIS**: blank garages facing the street in typical residential neighborhoods.
  ANTITHESIS: protruding bay windows on textured old Victorian homes.
- **THESIS**: the eye meets nothing but more street at the end of a block.
  ANTITHESIS: the eye looks down on the bay, or against a colorful facade of a T-junction.
- **THESIS**: from the sidewalk, you see parking lots leading to mini-malls or large shopping centers.
  ANTITHESIS: cafes, family-run groceries, fruit and vegetables.
- **THESIS**: sidewalks usually empty, business done by car.
  ANTITHESIS: consumers and service seekers flock to streets, the weird mixing with the normal.
- **THESIS**: neighborhoods are one-dimensional, either all commercial or all residential.
  ANTITHESIS: neighborhoods of varied textures where residence and commerce mix.
- **THESIS**: flat commercial facades, often windowless; no communication between buildings and street.
  ANTITHESIS: street murals; transparent windows link commerce to the street.

San Francisco is the antithesis. L.A. has a few exceptions to the thesis: Silver Lake, Venice, Pasadena, parts of Santa Monica and Echo Park, the funky east side of downtown. Could it be that San Francisco's residents simply decided to maintain their urbanscape on a human scale? Or does geography have something to do with it; the city is surrounded by water on three sides, so even if it did want to sprawl out, L.A. style, natural containment keeps it within liveable dimensions.

Self-contained neighborhoods back up against each other, each with its own history and character. Chinatown, Japantown, the Mission (Mexican and bohemian), the Castro's gay & lesbian community, wealthy Pacific Heights with its old Victorians, the touristy Fisherman's Wharf, Haight-Ashbury (the Haight), with its history of hippies and the San Francisco Mime Troupe, immense Golden Gate Park: arboreums, museums and athletic facilities, North Beach (the old beat habitat), and the newer SoMa (South of Market) for late night entertainment.

Real neighborhoods encourage walking and these communities are replete with public gathering places, outdoor cafes, parks, benches. Landmarks also motivate walkers, providing visible destinations: gardens in Golden Gate Park, murals and cafes in the Mission District, the Victorian mansions such as Haas-Lilienthal House, Octagon House or Spreckels Mansion in Pacific Heights, the Kabuki Hot Spring in Japantown, 710 Ashbury Street in the Haight (former communal home of the Grateful Dead), the Castro Theatre and cafes, Lawrence Ferlinghetti's City Lights Bookstore in North Beach.

San Francisco's Mission District murals make walking a true feast.

The hills add continuing wonder to the act of walking, Russian Hill with its famous Lombard Street switchback, Nob Hill with the Cable Car Barn. The three cable car routes, California St, Powell-Mason and Powell-Hyde, make a few connections between neighborhoods, especially to Fisherman's Wharf, with spectacular views of the bay. Buses link every other neighborhood (Municipal Transit Agency, 673-6864).

Pick up free timetables in bins on all buses and in public libraries. The Street and Transit Map is available for $2 in bookstores. The clearly marked BART subway and train system will get you anywhere in the larger Bay Area comfortably. A monthly MUNI Fast Pass covers all MUNI, CalTrain shuttles and BART within San Francisco limits, for only $35! With those rates, who needs a car?

When comparing living expenses in San Francisco and Los Angeles, consider the automobile variable. "Most people I know," said Gordon, a San Francisco resident, "don't even have cars." San Franciscan Peter Berg reminds us that "Ivan Illich calculated how much personal income is used to support an automobile - garage, gasoline, payments, repairs, insurance. Something like a quarter of personal income goes into automobiles. If you didn't have an automobile you wouldn't have to work one-quarter as much."

Less tangibly, by shopping in neighborhood stores and using public transportation, the average San Franciscan spends much more time in the public arena than the average L.A. resident, who drives alone and shops in a less personal context. Public gathering is a free form of entertainment. In its absence, one pays for more structured amusement.

Free street maps at airport information booths serve as guides for independent walking tours. Getting "lost" and finding one's way with guidance from local residents leaves room for the unexpected. Part of the fun of a good walk is not knowing everything in advance. Give serendipity a chance.

Newcomers may enjoy some of San Francisco's many organized walking tours. The Friends of the San Francisco Public Library (557-4266) offer a comprehensive package of free walking tours guided by knowledgable historians. Have a pen and paper ready when you call; the menu of walks and pick-up points on their recorded message is extensive.

Other walking tours with approximate prices: the "brothel stroll" with San Francisco Strolls (282-7924, $20); the Chinese Culinary Walk and Luncheon (986-1822, $30); Cruisin' the Castro (550-8110, $30); The Flower Power Haight-Ashbury Tour, painfully nostalgic for old hippies (221-8442, $15); the Mission District Mural Walk, vibrant street paintings replete with social symbolism in the spirit of the great Mexican muralists, Rivera, Orozco and Siqueiros (285-2287).

Angelinos who wish to simplify their existence can sell their two cars and move here. If no job materializes, they can survive in the underground economy for a fraction of what they'd need to earn in the mainstream down south. For lower rents, the streetwise can find a reasonable apartment in the less gentrified Mission District.

San Francisco vies with New Orleans for "most exciting city in the U.S.A." It's a close call, but after factoring in the sapping heat and humidity of summertime New Orleans, I'd opt for the more benign fresh weather of San Francisco. If you like it hot and steamy, New Orleans gets extra points.

This section is not intended as an all-encompassing, encyclopedic summary of San Francisco. Our objective is to highlight a stimulating context where one may evade the grand scheme of automobile determinism.

But lovers of street life, before you give up on L.A., allow Charles and Isabel the chance to prove that Angelinos who prefer a pedestrian-friendly existence need not quit, that with a little fighting spirit, a carless way of life is possible in L.A.

TO FIGHT

God put me here in L.A. to teach people how to live without an automobile.

—Charles Thomas

Nigel Sylvester first saw Charles on an L.A. bus. "He looked like an old Irish brawler, in a plaid hunter's jacket and sky blue cowboy boots." Nigel was returning home from Brentwood, from "the one job that became impossible." Nigel was a magazine editor at the time. Both men were raised in cities where driving was not necessary, Nigel in London, Charles in New York.

Nigel, a former university professor with a Ph.D., was reluctant to talk with "the brawler" during his long commute, "between an hour and a half and two hours each way."

Eventually Nigel and Charles became friends. Both feel uncomfortable driving. Both believe that the distances in Southern California are beyond the human scale.

"We used to go down to see my grandmother in Brighton," Nigel explains. "Brighton was 60 miles from London. For us it was like going to the end of the earth."

"Out here in the Valley they'd say Santa Monica is a 30-minute drive," Charles explains. "I'd say it's 50 miles away and it's not local. I have an eastern mindset about distance."

Eventually Nigel quit the gig in Brentwood and took a high school teaching position 15 to 20 minutes from his house by bus. Charles works in a government office in downtown L.A. and gets there by a freeway bus. Both read or chat on their rides and don't mind it at all.

Nigel met Cristina in California. After several children came along, Cristina convinced Nigel it was time to get a car.

Charles and Isabel also met in California. Isabel, a small woman with a big spirit, got rid of her car. "We live like kings," says Isabel, "because we don't have a car."

After four children, Nigel and Cristina admit that the car has become a necessity, but Nigel still won't drive. After they'd begun to

179

take their oldest daughter to horseback riding lessons in Pasadena, 20 miles away, their concept of distance was forever altered.

"It always amazed me the distances people were prepared to travel to go shopping or have lunch," Nigel laments. "We now travel to Pasadena to go to the supermarket."

So you've bought in to the Southern California ideology, I suggest.

"It's true we go distances," Nigel responds, "but I'd still prefer to use the bus. Nowadays, though, most people on buses are using stupid headphones. People no longer talk to each other. The people who still communicate on my bus route are the Hispanics going to work in the light industries.

"I never thought of adjusting or not adjusting. I don't like cars, I never did. But the reason a car became essential to us was because we had four children. With one child we went everywhere mainly walking, with the child in the stroller, taking occasional buses."

In those days, Nigel and Cristina had a perfect strategy to avoid the automobile culture. Nigel taught at the University of Southern California and Cristina worked at 32nd Street School right across from U.S.C. They lived only a few blocks from work. Today, they thrive with one car where comparable L.A. couples need two.

"It's sometimes frightening that I don't drive," Nigel admits. "If Cristina gets stuck on the freeway, I can't bop out and pick her up. We have to rely on a network of friends."

Charles looks like a brawler but he's sweet and charming on the inside. Isabel looks frail but she's tough as nails. Charles' confrontation with the automobile culture was made more demanding by a foot problem that required special shoes. He was not able to walk long distances.

That all changed when he quit smoking. Within a month, the nagging foot ailment had dissipated. Youth was a long time ago for both Charles and Isabel but that's only a chronological thing. Today, they've got the energy to walk incredibly long distances, for errands or recreation.

Prior to their walking renaissance, Charles had been in the hospital with diabetes. Isabel walked 15 miles to see him, nearly as far as Nigel and Cristina's drive to Pasadena. When he was released, Isabel resolved that she would not be injecting him with insulin for long. She studied the intricacies of nutrition and cured Charles through diet and exercise.

Today, both Charles and Isabel are crusaders against Southern California automobile determinism. Charles has submitted a bus plan to San Fernando Valley authorities and waits for a response. He gets heard in the newspapers, usually the *Daily News* and occasionally the *L.A. Times*.

In a letter to the *Times* that criticized the city's failure to address its transportation problems, Charles brought up the difference in way of life between New York and Los Angeles.

"I was born and raised on Manhattan Island," he wrote, "within walking distance of Times Square, and see the way of life there (the widespread use of public transportation) as normal and ideal. Angelinos tend to despise "Manhattanization" and to jealously defend one's God-given right to use an automobile whenever and however they please."

Charles defends L.A.'s costly metro rail and subway project and by implication criticizes his friend Nigel for allowing himself to be driven 20 miles to go shopping. Nigel is too self-critical. He still goes against the grain, busing to work and doing errands on foot.

Charles and Isabel are not the only Southern Californians who believe that the automobile culture has literally gone too far. Support grows for alternatives. But how much of the movement against automobile determinism comes from ex-New Yorkers? Native Southern Californians who hear Charles' arguments wonder what all the fuss is about. Why abandon the automobile? Science can find a way to minimize pollution without shattering their icon. The answer for them lies in experiments like electric cars or more benign alternative fuels.

Can Southern Californians be weaned away from seeing the automobile as a vital appendage of the human body? What if, after many billions go into a metro system, they decide not to use it?

That won't happen if Charles and Isabel have their way.

Chapter Nine

TRAVEL SMART

This chapter on survival skills includes those categories that lend themselves to narrative. An Interactive Directory at the end of the book will cover other vital information where phone numbers and/or addresses are of strategic value.

For handy reference, survival topics are listed in alphabetical order.

AIRPORTS

Compared to the unwieldy LAX in Los Angeles, Burbank Airport to the north is small and comfortable. The airport in San Francisco is less user-friendly than the smaller Oakland Airport across the bay. Most airlines fly out of both the large and small airports. If you have a choice and suffer from airport-phobia, Burbank and Oakland are the answer.

AUTOMOBILES

A new car depreciates as soon as it leaves the dealership. It is considerably more economical to buy a used car. Dealers sell both new and used cars and expect the potential client to bargain. Better opportunities may be found in newspaper ads by independent owners.

In buying a used car, you might be taking over someone else's headache. The recommended tactic: pay a qualified mechanic to have your potential purchase tested. If possible, find a mechanic by word of mouth, but as a last resort, ask at a service station.

The single most important maintenance requirement is the oil change. Ask the seller to show you his oil change receipts. If the car has had an oil change every 3,000 miles, it's more likely to be in good shape.

Fast in-and-out oil change outlets belonging to nationwide corporations such as Jiffy Lube usually do a good job, but the guys who change your oil there are trained only for that. Mechanics at any gas station with a garage will change your oil. If you get there early, you probably won't have to wait. Always ask about special sales on oil changes, tune-ups and brake work.

The single factor that makes a driver more vulnerable, to accidents and a police record, is alcohol. Hard drinkers should make sure they're accompanied by a "designated driver." In California it is illegal to operate a motor vehicle with a blood alcohol level of .08% or above. If you're stopped, the police have a right to test you. If you fail the test, you can be locked up. Seatbelts are also a requirement, as is liability insurance.

For road conditions, call toll free: 800-427-7623.

Well-known rent-a-car companies are in phone directories. Many smaller companies operate locally with lower rates. Rent-a-Wreck (800-421-7253) makes less attractive cars available for lower rates, unless you want to show off in an old Edsel or Mustang. That will cost you.

TIP: Beware of exorbitant daily insurance charges. If you anticipate renting a car, it is far less expensive to pay a yearly fee on your own insurance policy that covers rentals, especially for collision.

CONSUMERISM

Harvard author Juliet Schor writes that "we spend three to four times as many hours a year shopping as our counterparts in Western Europe."

Dazzled by megamalls, department stores, 24-hour supermarkets, and discount warehouses, some foreigners shop with more fervor than the natives. Converts make for the most fanatic believers. Here are a few pointers on smart shopping.

Yard Sales

On weekends, most neighborhoods have yard sales. The best of these are called "estate sales" or "moving sales," where good things are being unloaded. Wade through the mud to find the gold. Cheap used hardwood furniture can be superior to expensive new furniture at retail stores.

TIP: The more tenacious buyers from used furniture stores go to yard sales to obtain merchandise. When the sale is announced for 9:00 am, expect these vultures at 8:45. Don't take the listed hour on a posted announcement or newspaper ad literally. You don't want to be left with the carcasses.

Flea Markets

Every city and rural region has a good flea market. Flea market vendors constitute a fascinating subculture. The most famous flea market in California is the Rose Bowl Flea Market on the second Sunday of each month in Pasadena. It costs $10 to get in, but it's worth it. Phone 213-588-4411. Most flea markets are free; just ask around. Bargaining permitted.

Warehouses

Warehouse chains such as Price Club and Sam's Club offer discount prices if you buy in volume. These outfits are a suburban phenomenon, so you'll need a car to get there. One-time membership fees are nominal. Food, clothing, pharmaceuticals, electronics, and much more.

Garment Districts

Here you can find the same pieces of clothing you'd see in major department stores for a fraction of the price. Expect an exciting multicultural experience at the downtown Los Angeles garment district. (Walk east from Broadway on 11th Street and you won't miss it!)

Discount Chain Specialty Stores, Hardware, Office Supplies, etc.

It's getting harder to find a good old-fashioned hardware store with personal service. The corporate giants will save you more than a few bucks, but at what social cost?

Farmers' Markets. This institution allows you to buy fresh produce directly from the producer, thus avoiding the middle-man. Schedules change, as do neighborhoods. The best strategy: ask around.

Specialty stores. California immigrant communities create a honky tonk underground economy, typified by the eastern part of downtown L.A. and the Mission in S.F. Third World free enterprise at its best. Upscale specialty stores are more prevalent in San Francisco but are found in every California city.

CRIME

With so many ethnic groups in California, newcomers do not stick out; the visitor is less likely to be perceived as a wealthy tourist by muggers and con artists.

On the other hand, the crime rate in most American urban centers, including parts of L.A. and San Francisco, is higher than in comparable European cities.

I hesitate to stigmatize certain "dangerous" neighborhoods because, as one L.A.P.D. officer told me, crime may occur at any time in any place. My wife was attacked by a would-be rapist in a middle class neighborhood not known for its crime. Not a big woman, she fought off the brute.

His mistake: to overestimate her height and clamp his hands over her nose instead of her mouth, allowing her to scream. Her mistake: to take the inner part of the sidewalk home from college classes in the darkening day-end shadows of trees and hedges rather than walking on the outside of the sidewalk in view of passing motorists.

The key to personal safety is to greatly reduce the probability of any crime occurring, and to then minimize the probablity of bodily harm or death if a crime does occur. This is done by applying rules of common sense, not by staying cooped up in a boring neighborhood or walking around with a bulletproof vest.

Walking in the shadows of buildings and alleys instead of near the street increases vulnerability. Looking like you're lost sends a signal to a lurking mugger. Shopping at a one-clerk all-night convenience store at midnight leaves you more in the way of a potential incident than patronizing a well-frequented all-night supermarket. Jogging in a deserted park at 5:00 am is not smart.

If a guy with a gun demands your money, give it to him. Money is replaceable. (Don't take your whole stash with you.) If a man in a plaid sports jacket and dark glasses says he'll sell you the Golden Gate Bridge for only two thousand dollars, pass up the offer. When you feel you're being followed, step into a crowded restaurant or hail a taxi to the nearest commercial district.

DISNEYLAND

The lines are obscenely long. You get all the rides for a single park "passport," but long waits are annoying. On holidays and summer weekends, reliable sources report that they were only able to cover five rides, even when remaining throughout the day and evening.

Adding insult to injury are long lines for "fast" foods.

When finally reaching the building housing an attraction, one discovers that the line continues winding inside. (On prime-season weekends, the wait for Indiana Jones can be as long as three hours, and 45 minutes is a normal wait for other major attractions.)

TIP: On off-season weekdays, when the Southern California weather remains splendid, you can walk directly into rides with no waits, covering the whole park even though closing time is 6:00 pm instead of 9:00 pm summer closing. Under these circumstances, Disneyland is a pleasure.

TIP: Avoid the "It's a Small World" ride. As your car winds through a tunnel with dolls from different cultures popping out around each bend, a sappy sixteen-bar melody repeats, repeats, repeats. Once you are out of It's A Small World, the melody will follow you around for the rest of your life. Years later it will sneak into your shower, and creep into your mind as you try to meditate in the park.

In fairness to the original Disneyland of California, the summer lines at Orlando's Disneyworld are more uncomfortable in Florida's tropical humidity. At Disneyland and other theme parks like Magic Mountain in Valencia, the management is kind enough to spray a cool mist upon you as you wait in line.

"It makes you feel like a fern," commented Carlos, an efficiency expert.

Disneyland's Main Street USA celebrates with fabricated nostalgia the type of attractive main streets that were phased out in real life by developers like the Disney Corporation itself.

At this writing adults pay $34 for a California Disneyland passport, seniors $30, children from 3-11 $26. The passport allows unlimited use of all attractions except arcades. Parking costs extra. A family of two adults and two children will pay over $150 for the day after food and parking is factored in.

For recorded information, phone 714-999-4565. A toll-free call to 800-225-2057 will get you a free brochure.

EARTHQUAKES

In case of an earthquake, conventional wisdom dictates that you either stand under a door jamb or curl under a table. My patented solution: keep a table under a door jamb and get beneath both.

Sometimes quakes give a warning with a slow, rumbling crescendo. But most earthquakes won't allow you the time to react with precision; they start big and last only a few seconds.

During my first earthquake, I thought I'd been stricken with a bout of nausea. By the time I realized it was a quake, it was too late to take safety measures. As another big quake struck, my wife was driving to work and thought she'd had a flat tire. She was in good company. Other drivers reacted the same way, braking at the shoulder of the freeway, wondering why everyone was getting a flat tire at the same time in the same place.

Without much time to react, the best strategy is to keep your living quarters in a safe mode. Don't sleep beneath a shelf holding a bulky vase or you'll learn first hand about "flower power." Don't sleep next to a wall with a glass covered print of *Guernica*. Keep supplies such as extra food, a first aid kit, a battery-operated radio, a flash light. Know where the gas shut-off valve is, in case of a leak. Duck, cover, and hold on until the quake is over. You won't need a long attention span to wait it out. No quake has lasted more than 27 seconds since the 110-second San Francisco earthquake of 1906. (Damage is as much a function of duration as it is of intensity.)

Remain inside if you are inside, and outside if you are outside. In modern homes, doorways are no safer than anywhere else; a sturdy table is the best hiding place.

Earthquake heart atttacks may be caused by panic. Unless you are in an old adobe house, there is no reason to panic. Driving on the ice in Pennsylvania or sitting in the path of a tornado in Oklahoma is far more deadly. The best earthquake strategy is to stay calm.

FREE ENTERTAINMENT

Alphabetically, "Free Entertainment" is sandwiched somewhere between Disneyland and Gambling, two of the more expensive forms of amusement.

The subject of free entertainment in California deserves a whole guide. Outdoor art exhibitions, free concerts in parks, art galleries, and street fairs are all the norm, not the exception. Even the source of these events is free: the local throwaway newspaper. Here's a selected list.

Concerts

Every city and town has free concerts. Examples: Twilight Dance Concerts, July through August, blues, 50s music, etc., on the Santa Monica Pier, due west of L.A. where Interstate 10 hits the sea (310-458-8900). Alameda Park in Santa Barbara has Sunday concerts June through September, jazz, swing, reggae, etc., at 3:00 pm (805-962-8956).

Hot Springs

Tecopa Hot Springs, southeast of Death Valley National Monument, a desert oasis. Take a replenishing dip, five miles south of Shoshone, Highway 127 (619-852-4264).

Movie Stars in Action

The LA Film Permit Office supplies a listing of filming locations (213-485-5324).

Museums

Most museums are free one day per month. For example, the San Francisco Museum of Modern Art requires no fee on the first Tuesday of every month (151 Third St, 415-357-4000). The Griffith Park Observatory, Hall of Science, in L.A. is free at all times (north of

Vermont Avenue, 213-664-1191), as are the museums in Old Town
San Diego State Historic Park (Old Town exit off Interstate 5, 619-
220-5422).

Odds and Ends
The State's Oldest Operating Drug Store is in Weaverville, in an
historic district with a museum (from Interstate 5 north, take Highway
299 west, 916-623-5211).

- **The Grunion Run**. When grunion fish squirm onto the beach and
  attempt to spawn, you can catch them with your hands from March
  to August during a full new moon (Cabrillo Marine Aquarium,
  L.A. County, 310-548-7562).

- **Race Horse Workouts**. Clockers Corner. During the Santa Anita
  racing seasons, Octobers, and from December 26 through the last
  week of April, the early morning horse workouts are seen close up
  at Clockers Corner, right at the track, from 7:30 am through 9:30.
  (Get off Freeway 210 at the Baldwin exit in Arcadia). Nothing is
  more graceful than the flow of galloping thoroughbreds, some the
  descendents of the great Nureyev (the horse). Outdoor breakfast
  and espresso available.

Clockers' Corner morning workouts at Santa Anita Race track in Arcadia.

There are still great places to walk in Southern California and you can also benefit from the free entertainment along the way. Here, Andean musicians play in front of the Midnight Special Bookstore, 3rd street Promenade, Santa Monica.

- **Surfing Competition**, Huntington Beach State Park in Orange County, south of L.A. on Pacific Coast Highway 1, end of July/ beginning of August (310-286-3600).

- **TV Programs.** Fox TV Network's Box Office is open weekday work hours for free tickets to TV programs (5746 Sunset Blvd, 818-753-3470).

- **Walking Tours**. Every city has them. Examples: Old Town Sacramento, cobblestone streets and Gold Rush era buildings (916-442-7644). Yreka has 75 restored 19th century homes, also from the Gold Rush era (916-842-1649).

- **Wine Tasting** in Sonoma County, highway 101 north of San Francisco, with visitor's center maps in Rennert Park (5000 Roberts Lake Rd., 707-586-8100).

Other free activities are too spiritual to be considered "entertainment," and should be appreciated with due respect, especially in California's unlimited religious scene. One example suffices:

- **John Coltrane**. St. John's African Orthodox Church, 351 Divisadero, in San Francisco, holds services at 11:45 am on Sundays and 6 pm on Wednesdays in a converted storefront adorned with paintings of the great jazz saxophonist John Coltrane. Coltrane's inspired "A Love Supreme" and other compositions are the musical basis for these Catholic services. A St. John's nun cautioned me to not present her sanctuary as a place for curiosity seekers, since it represents devoted and traditional religious belief. Go here only if you believe as I do that Coltrane's music comes from divine inspiration.

Any discussion of "the best things in life are free" must end with California's superb beaches and coastline, a pantheist's delight.

GAMBLING

Three of the world's most interesting gambling havens border on California. To the northwest is the Nevada side of Lake Tahoe. On the southwest is Las Vegas, Nevada, forty miles from the California state line. To the south is Tijuana, Mexico.

The most conspicuous gaming machines and tables involve "negative expectation" gambling. Slot machines (one-armed bandits), roulette, craps, baccarat and keno have a fixed mathematical edge that favors the house to the inevitable detriment of the player. If you think it's fun to lose, play these games.

These same locations offer positive expectation gambling. Positive expectation refers to games like poker, sports and horse race betting whose return on investment depends on the knowledge and skill of the player, where a profit remains possible, even though most players lose.

In these more challenging games, the player actually competes against other players, with the house acting as a commissioned broker. Professionals advise that with sports betting, avoid parlays in which more than one of your teams must win in order for you to collect; only bet individual games, in which you have to lay out $11 dollars in order to win $10. The extra dollar "the vigorish" is the house's profit. If you bet 110 dollars on the San Francisco 49ers and they "beat the spread," you would collect $210.

American football is the most popular betting sport. The point spread works in a tricky way. Say the 49ers are favored by 6 points. In order for you to win, they must win by 7. If they win by 5 or less, you lose and the guy who bets their opponent wins. If they win by 6, it's a wash, and your bet is returned.

Horse betting permits the best chance for a profit. Casinos have "race books," with monitors of tracks across the country. Admission is free and there is sometimes a discount for racing forms with horses' past performances.

Gamblers Book Club (GBC) in Las Vegas does both walk-in and mail order business. Knowledgable staff will recommend the best books on horse race handicapping, sports betting, and poker. Phone: 800-634-6243.

Within California, there are two racing circuits, northern and southern. Golden Gate Fields is perched at the edge of the bay, just outside of Berkeley. In Southern California, the elegant Santa Anita is the most European of American tracks, with a pretty downhill turf course. Summers are at Del Mar by the sea, just north of San Diego. Distracted by bikini-clad women, one good handicapper squandered an entire bankroll at Del Mar.

Racing Forms are purchased in selected liquor stores and newstands. Other tracks include Hollywood Park in Inglewood (south of L.A.), Bay Meadows (south of San Francisco) and various state fairs for cheaper horses. (Off-track wagering facilities located at state fair facilities; legal casinos at Indian reservations.)

Lake Tahoe

Of these three gambling havens, Lake Tahoe is the most splendid, with an alpine lake, pine aromas, and hiking trails. Summers are fresh and cool. Snowy winters make it an ideal ski resort.

Tijuana

Tijuana has a superb cultural center. With the North American Free Trade Agreement, a growing Tijuana now has more than 700,000 inhabitants, many of whom are waiting for a chance to sneak across the border. Many Californians go there for inexpensive dental or automobile work, to eat lobster at Playas de Tijuana, or for the raucous dancing bars. Tijuana has perfect climate year round.

Las Vegas

Everyone has heard of Las Vegas, the gambling city built in the middle of the desert, where casinos light the night sky with gaudy motifs. Today, Las Vegas ha evolved into a family theme hotel city. It has urbanized to the extent where there are now gang problems. The world's most intelligent full-time gamblers live in Las Vegas, choosing gambling amenities and reduced overhead over aesthetics. Food is cheap.

Regular gamblers ignore the town's glitzy shows. Las Vegas is pleasant in the winter, but from the end of spring to early autumn, temperatures may rise as high as 118°F (nearly 50°C), with only the zero humidity saving one's life. Needless to say, the casinos are all air conditioned. One big winner in Las Vegas is the electric company.

HEALTH CARE

The private health care system in the U.S., burdened by the overhead of fancy technology and a baroque network of insurance middlemen, is quite expensive. The total population of most countries in the world is lower than the population of uninsured inhabitants in the U.S.A. Visitors from abroad have the option of taking out comprehensive travel insurance before they leave or winging it.

A growing contingent of independent professionals not attached to a "group" insurance policy have become refugees from formal health care and practice rigid preventive medicine, avoiding high-risk habits like smoking or fat consumption, and engaging in regular exercise of aerobic value such as fast walking, running, swimming and bicycling.

The standard formula for a healthy diet (plenty of fruits, vegetables and grains) is elaborated upon in magazines such as *Prevention*, whose circulation goes up with every rise in the cost of health care. Thanks to important legislation, packaged food is now fully labeled, so cautious eaters who wish to control fat, sugar or sodium intake know exactly what they get. Preventive health experts advise us to avoid processed foods such as TV dinners and canned goods, which lose in nutritional value and gain in questionable additives.

Virtually every community has quarter-mile running tracks, tennis and basketball courts and other free athletic amenities. If you're strictly in it for health and enjoyment, there is no need to join a trendy health club. In other words, if one wishes to stay fit in the U.S.A., and especially in health-conscious California, the facilities are there. California weather lends itself to healthy pleasures like bicycling, hiking and walking.

The most expensive institution in the whole system is the hospital emergency room. If you have any reason to know in advance that you will be needing care, make arrangements with a local clinic or hospital. Some communities have "free clinics" in which one is asked to make a donation according to one's means. Major hospitals connected with universities have programs that charge according to ability to pay. Other hospitals have urgent care clinics whose cost is relatively lower than what you'd pay in an emergency room.

California is a leading state in the arena of alternative medicine. The best source for information on local clinics, alternative specialists and other health facilities is the nearest health food store bulletin board.

LIBRARIES

In this age of privatization, thus far no politician has dared to suggest privatizing American public libraries, quite possibly the best in the world. County and city public library systems in California have lots of amenities, including a superb collection of books on California.

Other features include:

- Easy-to-use data bases of magazine and newspaper articles, with key-word indexes. When a full text is available, you can print it out free of charge.
- If the article or book you're looking for is not in stock, they'll search for it elsewhere in the system and have it brought in within a week.
- Free access to the internet, excluding E-mail.
- Public libraries sponsor free events for children.
- Also: maps, coin-operated typewriters, helpful reference librarians.

PHONING FOR INFORMATION

At one time, a phone call was a quicker way of obtaining information than going in person. This is changing as more and more public and private services have recorded voice mail or answering devices.

"If you'd like XXX press 1, if you'd like YYY, press 2," etc. After you've pressed 3 to talk with ZZZ, you may get a whole new menu. Sometimes none of the menu offerings are precisely what you want. Other times you need to speak to an operator and nothing on the menu allows you to do so.

Sometimes a long distance bill is run up listening to menus. It's a gold mine for the phone companies. These answering devices represent an attempt by Americans to become even further insulated from direct personal contact.

There are two strategies for dealing with answering devices. The first: press the most general menu option so that the person responding will not tell you "Oh, I'm sorry, I deal with the stegasaurus, you need to speak to the number that deals with the brontasaurus."

The best strategy is to heed the final message: "If you have a rotary phone please stay on the line and an operator will assist you." I don't have a rotary phone but I've been able to reach a human being this way.

PHOTOGRAPHY

California, especially in the southern region, receives nearly double the amount of daylight as New York. In the interest of sharpness, outdoor pictures are best taken in the early morning or late afternoon.

People do not look kindly on being photographed close up without prior permission, although no one seems to complain when they are part of an overall street scene.

POSTAL SERVICE

Many Americans complain about their postal service. They haven't lived in other countries. As a writer I depend on the post office and I've become quite patriotic about a service that has never let me down.

TIP: You can use a special two-day mail pouch, available at no cost on post office premises, and cram as much into it as you like, under two pounds, for only $3. At this writing, it costs 32 cents for a letter within the U.S.A. and 60 cents to mail one abroad. That's cheaper than in countries with a significantly lower cost of living than the U.S.A.

PROSTITUTION

Prostitution is illegal in California. Getting caught with a streetwalker is only advised if you think the publicity will advance your career. When driving in the area of Sunset or Hollywood Boulevards between

Normandie and Vine, don't let streetwalkers distract your driving. Some of them might be undercover cops and others could be cross dressers.

Prostitution is legal south of the border and in every county of Nevada except for the Las Vegas and Reno regions. Don't fall for prostitution scams in Las Vegas, where you'll likely be separated from your money with nothing in return.

In areas where prostitution is legal, sexual workers must submit to periodic testing for AIDS and venereal deseases. But they are not tested after each client, so the threat of AIDS should be discouragement enough.

RESTAURANTS

California has thousands of superb restaurants and eating stands. Ever since my favorite bistro was left out of Paris travel guides, I decided that naming individual restaurants is not as helpful as outlining strategies for finding them.

TIP: One-of-a kind family-run Mexican restaurants are far superior to any of the upscale spots. Apply the *"mole"* test (pronounced "moley"). A Mexican restaurant is authentic if it has *mole* on the menu. *Mole* is a chicken dish with a dark sauce made of mildly hot peppers and a dash of chocolate. If no *mole* is on the menu, you're much less likely to be dealing with authentic Mexican food.

Try Juan's Mexican restaurant in West Berkeley, a real neighborhood hangout. Also try the *"al pastor"* taco stand test. If they have *"tacos al pastor"* (pork from a turning rotisserie wrapped in corn tortillas), they're the real thing.

For most Chinese restaurants, the lunch menu offers the same dishes for significantly less. This is true for other types of restaurants as well. In most countries I've lived in, one's larger meal is served at midday. Americans tend to have their big meal at night. If you eat out a lot, your budget will stretch by making lunch the main meal.

When in the Chinatown of any city (San Francisco's is the most famous), try restaurants where the menu is in Chinese only. You enhance the probability of getting something authentic, although you may not know what you've asked for.

In health-conscious California, many restaurants include tasty vegetarian dishes on their menu. All-you-can-eat salad bars offer an ideal way to fill up without fattening up. You may inspect the salad bar to see if it has the goodies you want. Some salad bars allow for a good measure of creative combinations, with sunflower seeds, pastas, kiwis, home-made breads, and other surprises.

One improves the odds of choosing a good Italian restaurant if the sign says New York Italian food. Miceli's, on Cahuenga Boulevard in Universal City (L.A. County), does not use the New York strategy, but instead has singing waiters and waitresses. Murals of Italian villages add to the atmosphere.

For a night on the town, one custom is to eat out and then go to hear music or dance. Why not combine the two stages into one, Miceli style, choosing a no-cover-charge restaurant that provides entertainment for the price of the food. Restaurant listings in newspapers will state whether or not there is a cover charge.

La Bamba on Raymond Street in Pasadena typifies this type of all-purpose establishment: superb Caribbean-Cuban food and live salsa music.

Tipping

Tipping is not complicated. At restaurants, tip servers 15% of your bill, provided that you are served at a table. Add an extra 5% if the service is beyond the call of duty. Be aware that restaurant servers get paid lower salaries as reverse compensation for their tips. There is no tipping at fast-food, takeout and buffet restaurants, but you're not supposed to leave a mess behind.

Taxi drivers get 10%, hairdressers 15%, skycaps or bellboys receive a dollar for the first bag and 50 cents for each additional piece of luggage. At some luxury hotels, everybody who gives you a smile expects a tip.

SPECTATOR SPORTS

The most popular spectator sports are professional "American" football (NFL) and basketball (NBA), their college equivalents, and major league baseball. Ice Hockey is also an expanding business.

Major League Soccer (MLS), what the rest of the world calls football, has finally taken a foothold.

Some of these private teams are subsidized by taxpayer money, yet charge exhorbitant amounts for tickets. Games are usually sold out for the San Francisco 49ers (football), the L.A. Lakers (basketball) and the L.A. Kings (ice hockey). University football and basketball teams provide substantial income for the institutions and yet the players, hopeful of landing pro contracts, gladly play without a salary, accepting athletic scholarships instead.

The most democratic spectator sport, and the one where tickets are easier to come by and less expensive, is baseball. It seems as if foreigners either love or hate baseball, whose meditative pace is punctuated with spurts of dramatic action.

There is a surcharge when purchasing tickets from middlemen like Ticket Masters. For most L.A. Dodgers, California Angels (Anaheim), Oakland As and San Francisco Giants baseball games, one can arrive the day of the game and find tickets.

TIP: One of the keys to deciphering U.S. culture may be found in baseball, especially with the importance it attaches to byzantine statistics and complex game-stopping strategies.

TIP: No matter how often we are reminded that "scalping" (reselling) tickets is illegal, ticket scalpers hang out around stadiums and arenas prior to games, and aren't very surreptitious about it. For a big game in which tickets are sold out, if one waits until after the opening kickoff or first pitch, scalpers with leftover tickets are willing to unload at reduced costs, sometimes even below the regular price if they're desperate. (Warning: there is some risk in buying from a scalper.)

INTERACTIVE DIRECTORY

This directory provides strategic information for enriching your stay in California. Inflation has been under control for quite some time but prices should be considered approximations, and phone numbers may occasionally change.

TOLL-FREE INFORMATION
Any business or organization with a toll-free 800 number can be located by calling the 1-800-555-1212 information number. When dialing an 800 number, or any long distance number, always dial 1 first. The obligatory 1 is not included in the list of phone numbers.

THROW-AWAY NEWSPAPERS
Every city and town has free weekly "throw-aways" replete with information on apartment rentals, apartments to share, used items for sale from cars to furniture, restaurants, music, clubs and dancing. Available in libraries, bookstores and convenience stores.

CHEAP TRAVEL

The Sunday travel pages of the nearest major newspaper *(L.A. Times, San Francisco Chronicle)* contain ads from discount travel agents and consolidators who buy tickets at bulk rate and sell them back to you non-refundable but with significant discounts. Make reservations on heavy travel days a day in advance of your required arrival and you may be fortunate enough to get "bumped." In such a case, the airline schedules you for the next available flight and gives you a free travel voucher for another flight, food vouchers, and free lodging if a stayover is necessary.

Driveaways

Sunday travel sections and phone directory Yellow Pages also run ads for "driveaways" under Auto Transporters and Drive-Away Companies. If you're lucky, a driveaway company may need a driver for an automobile going precisely to your destination; you must deliver the car within a prescribed period of time. There's enough leeway to tour along the way. Driveaways require a valid driver's license and a cash deposit (averaging $200 for cross country trips), which you recover upon delivery of the car. Letters of reference help, especially for those with foreign drivers licenses. You pay nothing but the gas, and you are given the car with a full tank. The company pays the expensive insurance, a great advantage over rental cars. On increasingly rare occasions when the company cannot match a destination with a driver, you may luck out with a gas allowance. Selected companies include: AAAdvantage Auto Transport (800-480-1733), Auto Transport and Driveaway (800-466-6935), Auto Driveaway (800-869-1489) and National Auto Transport (800-225-9611).

Other Key Travel Links

For any transportation, always ask for specials or discount fares. You'd be surprised how often you'll find discount promotions, especially with advance reservations and non-refundable tickets. Bus (Greyhound) and rail (Amtrak) have periodic long-term deals, from two-weeks to a month, allowing you unlimited travel for a single fare. Space is limited so it's a must to arrange well in advance.

AIRLINES: America West, 800-235-9292. American, 800-433-7300. Continental, 800-525-0280. Delta, 800-221-1212. Southwest, 800-435-9792 (this airline usually has the best rates within California). United, 800-241-6522. USAir, 800-428-4322.

BUS: Greyhound, 800-231-2222.

TRAIN: Amtrak, 800-872-7245.

The Green Tortoise

Gardner Kent is the hippest tour operator in California. The buses are stripped, bunks and mattresses replacing uncomfortable seats. No need for interior toilets; the tortoise stops frequently. The people-oriented trip is more important than the destination. The 20-30 crowd is a majority, but they've got grandmothers and baby boomers, too. Two thirds of the clients are foreign adventurers, mainly European. Communal eating and lots of social exchange make this anything but a normal bus ride.

Trips are one way because they cater to seasoned travelers who are not on a schedule. "The airlines are kicking the shit out of us with their price wars," says Gardner Kent, "but we're still doing well."

San Francisco to L.A. is $30, "and it's stayed that way for years," Kent adds. San Francsico to anywhere in Oregon is $39. They stop at what Kent calls "simulated state parks." A new Death Valley tour is $119 plus $31 for park admission, including gourmet food.

Write Gardner Kent at 494 Broadway, San Francisco, CA 94133, or toll free at 800-8678647, or 415-956-7500 in the San Francisco area.

RESTAURANTS
See **Survival Skills** (Chapter Nine).

HOTELS, MOTELS AND HOSTELS

Hotels and motels, with no cooking facilities, can deplete a bankroll. Major newspapers and the smaller weekly throw-aways occasionally run ads for house sitting, where the rent is free. For those who settle down in an apartment or home, lodging info is still important at vacation time.

Budget motel chains offer clean, relatively inexpensive rooms. Family operated motels are even less expensive by a few dollars, with no difference in quality of service.

Motel 6 (800-466-8356), is the most generic of motel chains. A room with double occupancy averages about $36. It could go up to the $50 range in San Francisco, while in small markets could cost in the mid twenties. Subtract about $6 for a single.

TIP: around the corner from a Motel 6 will usually be a less expensive family-owned motel, often run by foreigners, with rooms comparable to Motel 6. Rates may go up on weekends.

Hampton Inn (800-426-7866) has more amenities: free continental breakfast buffet with a variety of items and free local phone calls (most hotels hit you with a substantial surcharge for phone calls). Double occupancy costs you about $90 in important markets but as low as $55 in less touristy places.

Whale Watching Inns.

A little hedonistic, but on cold North Coast days, why not whale watch from your bed: binoculars provided.

Little River Inn (707-937-5942) the cheapest of whale watching hotels: $85 to $195.

Heritage House (800-235-5885), 1877 New England-style farmhouse, also in Little River. For an extra hundred or so, they throw in breakfast and dinner.

Towns of Albion, Elk and Gualala also have whale watching inns. The least expensive: Elk Cove Inn (800-275-2967), from $98 to $188 including a filling breakfast.

For a contrast from ocean bluffs, try the cheap California desert motels, on the border with Nevada and Arizona. This forgotten corner is a haven for drifters and the down and out. Weekly rates for Budget No. 1 Motel or the Desert Inn Motel, both in Needles, California, are less than the daily rates of whale watcher inns, but the people are more "interesting." Needles is where the Okies, in the 1930s on Route 66, entered the California desert in search of the promised land. John Steinbeck's Tom Joad called it "Murder Country" in *The Grapes of Wrath*.

Hostels

Most Americans don't know about U.S. hostels. Hostelling International-American Youth Hostels (800-444-6111) accepts reservations by credit card. HI-AYH's guide, *Hostelling U.S.A.* is available for free at any HI-AYH hostel, or for $3 by mail (Hosteling International, 733 15th St. N.W., Suite 840, Washington, D.C. 20005.)

The rates for selected hostels listed below range from $14 to $16 per night. You don't have to be a youth to get a bunk. Private rooms cost more.

- Eel River Redwoods Hostel in Leggett: 707-925-6425, $15.
- Hostelling International—Fisherman's Wharf, San Francisco:415-771-3645, $15.
- Pigeon Point Lighthouse, Pescadero: 415-879-0633, $14.
- Point Montara Lighthouse, Montara: 415-728-7177, $14.
- SLO Coast Hostel, San Luis Obispo: 805-544-4678, $16.
- Hostelling International—Santa Monica, Santa Monica: 310-393-9913, $19.

TIP: Gardner Kent's new Green Tortoise guest house is $15 during winters and $17 in the summer. Winters are mild in San Francisco, and this hostel adds an array of quirky amenities during the off-season, including pool (billiard) competition, special free beer nights, free Tuesday night dinners, free breakfasts, and other interactive events. Kent calls it a "party hostel." Phone: 415-834-1000.

SPECIALTY CLUBS AND ORGANIZATIONS

*I don't want to belong to any club that would have me as
a member.*

—Groucho Marx

Friendships are less likely to emerge from casual encounters. Visitors
are thus encouraged to join an organization where like-minded people
are bound to meet. More than 80% of Americans belong to some
organization!

Space constraints limit us to a selected list of clubs and organizations with open memberships. Should you not find a club or group
here that fits your affinities, heed the following:

TIP: The reference desk at public libraries has the *SourceBook*, a
compilation of local clubs and organizations, referenced by theme.

TIP: Local bookstores are an excellent source for leaflets an-
nouncing events sponsored by community organizations or local
branches of national ones. You'll readily tell from the event whether
people with persuasions similar to yours will be attending; most of
these events have a table where new members are recruited.

With these ideas in mind, lets look at a sampling of some of the
more bizarre California organizations. Number of members abbrevi-
ated after entry (eg. 2K is 2,000). Phone numbers in parentheses.
Sources for these clubs: word of mouth, regional source books, and
Organized Obsessions by Deborah M. Burek and Martin Connors
(Detroit: Visible Ink Press), "a perfect book for people looking for
that special group to join" and an alternative to the cyber-friendships
of the internet.

(Omitted are sectarian political and religious groups. If you
already belong to such an organization in your own state or country,
you will have no trouble finding an affiliated group in California.)

* **Abundantly Yours**. Motto: "Being the best you are regardless of
  size." Debunks myths about fat people. Sponsors participatory
  activities for the overweight, and an annual comedy-variety event.
  2K. PO Box 151134, San Diego, CA 92115 (619-286-4206).

207

- **Alliance for Survival**, a peace activist organization. Latest issue involves protest against war toys. Check 2035 4th St, Apt 103, Santa Monica, CA 90405 for other California branches. (310-399-1000).

- **Amalgamated Flying Saucer Clubs of America**. To inform the public about "the reality of flying saucers (extraterrestrial space-craft piloted by advanced men and women from other planets and star systems) and of their plan for imparting their advanced knowledge to the people of the earth." 5K. PO Box 39, Yucca Valley, CA 92286 (619-365-1141).

- **Art Dreco Institute**. Artists, art dealers, historians. To improve the reputation of "bad taste" Disregards public fashion. 250. 1709 Sanchez, San Francisco, CA 94131 (415-647-7532).

- **Audobon Society**. Prestigious environmental organization with many branches. Check 7377 Santa Monica Blvd, Los Angeles, CA 90046 for other California branches. (213-876-0202).

- **Bikers Against Manslaughter**. To reduce number of motorcycle accidents. Assistance in repairs, housing, and transportation. 100K. 5455 Wilshire Blvd., Room 1600, Los Angeles, CA 90036 (213-932-1277).

- **Bread and Roses**. Volunteer entertainers and caring people donate time and talent to folks in convalescent homes, prisons and psychiatric wards who "desperately need and appreciate the pleasure and human contact that live entertainment can bring." 78 Throckmorton Ave, Mill Valley, CA 94941.

- **California Trout**. To protect rivers, streams, trout, salmon, and watersheds (see interview in Ch. 6). Welcomes volunteers. 870 Market Street, Suite 859, San Francisco, CA 94102 (415-392-8887).

- **Cannabis Buyers Club of San Francisco**. California Attorney General Dan Lundgren shut down the CBC just before the November 1996 vote on legalizing marijuana for medical use

(Proposition 215). Prop 215 passed by a large majority, and CBC is back in action. (Ask around for new location.) This club has operated with the tacit approval of local authorities since 1991, providing marijuana for medical purposes only.

- **Count Dracula Society**. "Devoted to the serious study of horror films and Gothic literature. 300. 334 W 54th St, Los Angeles, CA 90037 (213-752-5811).

- **Crystal Stargate**. "Craft and wiccan practitioners, users of nature magic, and individuals interested in the psychic and supernatural." New Age. 150. PO Box 1761, San Marcos, CA 92069 (619-741-8148).

- **Earth First**. Militant environmentalists. See phone directory for latest location.

- **Earth Save**. Promotes ecology and dietary choices that are best for the environment. 706 Frederick St, Santa Cruz, CA 95060 (408-423-4069).

- **Eleventh Commandment Fellowship**. Open to all faiths. Practises the Eleventh commandment: "The earth is the Lord's and the fullness thereof; thou shalt not despoil the earth nor destroy the life thereon." 4K PO Box 14667, San Francisco, CA 94114 (415-626-6064).

- **Elves', Gnomes', and Little Men's Science Fiction, Chowder and Marching Society**. For S.F. lovers. PO Box 1169, Berkeley, CA 94701 (415-848-0413).

- **Exotic Dancers League of America**. "The striptease is an original American Art." Promotes this "fine old American tradition" and opposes pornography. 650. 29053 Wild Road, Helendale, CA 92342 (619-243-5261).

- **Fair-Witness Project**. Investigates the paranormal cases of "high-strange singularity." 500. 4219 W. Olive St. Suite 247, Burbank, CA 91505 (213-463-0542).

- **Flat Earth Research Society International**. "Dedicated to communicating evidence supporting the theory that the earth is flat." This iconoclast group believes that science is just another cult, and searches for the "plane truth." High desert location makes sense. 3K. Box 2533, Lancaster, CA 93539 (805-727-1635).

- **Food Not Bombs**, San Francisco anarchist group dedicated to feeding the homeless. Members spend time in jail after disobeying authorities about proper food distribution. No phone available.

- **Free Territory of Ely-Chatelaine**. Alliance of households declaring themselves free, autonomous states. Members believe that nation-states are obsolete, and prefer democratically-elected monarchical governments. 120. PO BOX 7075, Laguna Niguel, CA 92607 (714-240-8472).

- **Gold Prospectors Association of America**. A must if you're thinking of searching for gold in an environmentally compatible way. 84K. PO Box 507, Bonsall, CA 92003 (619-728-6620).

- **Greenpeace**. Internationally renowned group of committed environmental activists. Check 8599 Venice Blvd Ste A, Los Angeles, CA 90034 for other branches in California (310-287-2210).

- **Hollywood Studio Collectors Club**. A movie memorabilia business that encourages trading, buying and selling among its members. 9K 3960 Laurel Canyon Blvd, Suite 450, Studio City, CA 91614 (818-990-5450).

- **Horseless Carriage Club of America**. In the state where new and modern eclipsed old and traditional, old car hobbyists abound. 4.7K. 128 S. Cypress St, Orange, CA 92666 (714-538-HCCA).

- **Institute for the Development of the Harmonious Human Being**. Zen and other ancient teachings of spiritual revival and personal transformation. PO Box 370, Nevada City, CA 95959.

- **International Dull Men's Club**. Women's auxiliary: **Plain Janes**. "Recognition for the unrecognized, refuge and support in spirit for those who are not born charismatic, respect for the wise and humble among us who have led lives of accomplishment without arrogance." Not so dull! 650. 300 Napa St, No 10, Sausalito, CA 94965 (415-332-8190).

- **International Maledicta Society**. Interdisciplinary research into the language of verbal aggression and pejorative statements in all cultures. 3K. PO Box 14123, Santa Rosa, Ca 95402 (414-542-5853).

- **Laugh Lovers**. Promotes humor and laughter in daily living. PO Box 1495, Pleasanton, CA 94566 (415-462-3470).

- **Lovers of the Stinking Rose**. Garlic lovers, herbalists, organic gardeners, followers of alternative medicine. Annual Garlic Festival on July 14. 3K. 1621 Fifth St, Berkeley, CA 94710 (415-527-5175).

- **Names Project Foundation**. Ongoing creation of memorial patchwork quilt, "appropriate, compassionate response" to the AIDS epidemic, a medium of expression for people whose lives have been touched by AIDS. 2362 Market St, San Francisco, CA 94114 (415-863-5511).

- **National Association for the Advancement of Time**. Opposes nostalgia trends, seeks to "reestablish interest in the near future. Media entrenchment in the past throttles creativity today. Celebrates "Boycott the Past Week." 400. 6201 Sunset Blvd, Suite 114, Hollywood, CA 90028 (213-936-9876).

- **National Hobo Association**. To preserve the vagabond lifestyle and hobo literature. With everyone on the road, don't expect gatherings more than once a year. 2.5K. World Way Center, Box 90430, Los Angeles, CA 90009 (213-645-1500).

- **National Organization Taunting Safety and Fairness Everywhere (NOTSAFE)**. See Ch 4 on safety mania. Founder Dale Lowdermilk warns: "when you smell a flower you are putting your nose near the sexual organs of another species." Libertarians against government regulations. 1.4K. PO Box 5743EA, Montecito, CA 93150 (805-969-6217).

- **National Task Force on Prostitution**, *also called* **COYOTE (Call Off Your Tired Old Ethics)**. To decriminalize prostitution and "the removal of stigmas associated with female sexuality." 333 Valencia St, Suite 101, San Francisco, CA 94103 (415-558-0450).

- **Naturists and Nudists Opposing Pornographic Exploitation (NOPE)**. One of several groups whose newsletter is called "Iconoclast". Defends clothing-optional way of life, fights corporate exploitation of human sexuality. PO Box 2085, Rancho Cordoba, Ca 95741 (408-427-2858).

- **Overachievers Anonymous**. A self-help group for workaholics and others who are too driven. 10K. 1777 Union St, San Francisco, CA 94123 (415-928-3600).

- **People, Food and Land Foundation**. Small farmers and consumers unite to save water by developing arid land crops and other ecologically sound farming techniques. Self-healing, shamanism, ways to cook native plants. 500. 35751 Oak Springs Dr, Tollhouse, CA 93667 (209-855-3710).

- **Planetary Citizens**. Think local, act global. One Earth, One Humanity, One Destiny. Expand the U.N. 200K. PO Box 1509, Mt. Shasta, CA 96067.

- **Puppeteers of America**. Amateurs and professionals. 2K. 5 Cricklewood Path, Pasadena, CA 91107.

- **Radical Women. Socialist Feminists**. 523-A Valencia St, San Francisco, CA 94110 (415-864-1278).

- **Rat, Mouse and Hamster Fanciers**. Breeding and competitive events. 1756 14th Ave, San Francisco, CA 94122 (415-564-6374).

- **Route 66 Association**. Recreate the sense of discovery and romance that was typified by the old Route 66 highway. 300. PO Box 5323, Oxnard, CA 93031 (805-485-9923).

- **Sarcastics Anonymous**. For people who lose friends by uncalled for sarcasm and ridicule. Promotes positive uses of humor. 300. PO Box 1495, Pleasanton, CA 94566 (415-462-3470).

- **Sexaholics Anonymous**. PO Box 300, Simi Valley, CA 93062 (805-581-3343).

- **Sierra Club**. Prestigious environmental organization. Check 3345 Wilshire Blvd, Suite 508, Los Angeles, CA 90010 for other California branches. (213-387-4287).

- **Society for Creative Anachronism**. Re-enact medieval customs such as music, cooking and martial arts (they don't mention torture). 17K. PO Box 360743, Milpitas, CA 95036 (415-428-1181).

- **Somatics Society**. Mind control for better health. 800. 1516 Grant Ave, Suite 220, Novato, CA 94945 (415-897-0336).

- **Sons of the Desert**. Scholarly and social organization studying the characters and films of Laurel and Hardy. "The Way Out Tent" is the L.A. Branch which meets every six weeks. 5K. PO Box 8341, Universal City, CA 91608 (818-985-2713).

- **TreePeople**. Volunteers plant trees throughout Los Angeles, engage in environmental problem solving, programs in elementary schools. 20K. 12601 Mulholland Dr, Los Angeles, CA 90210 (818-753-4600).

CONTINUING EDUCATION COURSES

Ivan Illich has written that non-credit adult education is "much more effective than the best of formal schooling."

TIP: Continuing education departments at local community colleges are a superb medium for people of common persuasions to get

213

together. Courses are non-credit, so only motivated people register. Tuition is low compared to similar courses at university extentions. The philosophy is life-long learning, so there's no age segregation. Courses do not last a whole semester; short-term visitors confronting the estrangement of tourism can become part of a community by registering in courses that may last from a week to three months.

I've watched friendships develop in continuing education courses I've taught. One of my most challenging students, Jim, was dying of cancer. For many months after the course had ended, class companions would visit him, up until the time of his death.

They say that death is the great equalizer, but a common educational goal is a better equalizer. Within my classes, I observed a phenomenal degree of crosscultural rapport. And why not? Asians, Africans, blacks, whites, Hispanics and Middle Easterners all shared a common interest.

The United States is in the vanguard of continuing education, and California community colleges offer the most eclectic (and the most non-traditional) subjects. What follows is a selected list of direct phone numbers to some of the best continuing education programs.

- American River College, Sacramento. 916-484-8643
- City College of San Francisco. 415-267-6523
- College of the Redwoods, Eureka. 707-445-6195
- Laney College, Oakland. 510-464-4242
- Long Beach City College. 310-599-8124
- Los Angeles City College. 213-953-4204
- Napa Valley College, Napa & St. Helena. 707-967-2900, X2911.
- Orange Coast College, Orange County. 714-432-5880
- Pasadena City College. 818-585-7601
- San Diego College. 619-527-5258
- Santa Barbara College. 805-687-0812
- Santa Monica College. 310-452-9214

HIKING AND BACKPACKING

Anywhere in California, you're never far from superb trails. If you're just out for the exercise, ask for the nearest state park. If you wish to trek in a group, the California Division of Tourism (916-322-2881) will provide a free list of Back Packing and Hiking Tours.

Abide by the obvious backcountry ethics, and any local rules in handouts on particular hikes. Use biodegradable soap and do your cleaning far removed from rivers or lakes. Bury human waste. Staying on the trail will not only help protect the environment but will keep you safe and clear from poison oak, rattle snakes, mud slides, and other hazards.

Public libraries have maps of state and national parks. Space only allows for a selected list of ideal for hikes.

- **Ansel Adams Wilderness Area**, 209-297-0706, rugged, be-tween Yosemite and Mono Lake. No need for a camera. Ansel's taken all the best shots.

- **Border Field State Park**, 619-575-3613, near Mexican border, natural marine estuary. See the Border Patrol action.

- **Death Valley National Park**, 619-786-2331. For desert lovers only.

- **Desolation Wilderness Area**, 619-573-2694. Pine trees and alpine lakes. Southwestern shore of Lake Tahoe.

- **Emerald Bay State Park**, 916-525-7277, rugged, pine tree terrain bordering on alpine Lake Tahoe, with Vikingsholm Mansion. This author's favorite place for romantic joy and meditative calm.

- **Golden Gate**, 415-556-2920, with great shoreline. Bay Area.

- **Humboldt Redwoods**, 707-946-2409, includes the Avenue of the Giants. North Country.

- **John Muir Wilderness Area**, 209,297,0706. Muir was the beloved pioneer of this high sierra, and California back country in general. He remains an inspiration for nature lovers and environmentalists.

215

- **Kings Canyon National Park**, 209-335-2856. Canyon, sequoia trees.

- **Lassen Volcanic National Park**, 916-595-4444. Active volcano and boiling lakes and streams.

- **Malibu Creek**, 818-880-0350 or 800-533-7275. Santa Monica Mountains, Los Angeles.

- **Mount Diablo State Park**, 510-837-2525. Spectacular views. Bay Area.

- **Mount Tamalpais State Park**, Marin County north of San Francisco, extraordinary panoramas of the Pacific Ocean, San Francisco, and the bay. An hour's drive from San Francisco.

- **Natural Bridges State Beach**, 408-423-4609, with monarch butterflies in the winter.

- **Pacific Coast Trail**, the Pacific Coast Trail Association, 800-817-2243. Hiking 15 miles a day, you can make it from Border Field Park on the Mexican border to the Oregon border in about four months.

- **Placerita Canyon County Park**, 805-259-7721, north of L.A. on the way to the high desert.

- **Point Reyes National Seashore**, 415-663-1092. Bay Area.

- **Redwood National Park**, 707-464-6101, include's the world's largest redwood.

- **Sequoia National Park**, 209-565-3134, includes Mt. Whitney, the highest peak in the lower 48 states, 14,494 feet. Well-cared-for mountaineers route for non-pros. Don't climb during rain/snow season. Prepare for the altitude by getting in good shape before the climb. Eat lightly, move slowly as soon as you feel the altitude, and take periodic rests and deep breaths. If you still get altitude sickness, the best cure is immediate descent, with aspirin alleviating the discomfort.

- **Sinkyone Wilderness**, 707-986-7711, if you like it primitive. North Country.
- **Sonoma Coast**, 707-875-3483, north of San Francisco.
- **Yosemite National Park**, 209-372-0264, waterfalls, giant sequoias, glacier-carved valley, rock-climbing. If you only hike in one place, this should be it.

Topographic Maps

Once they've decided on their adventure location, serious trekkers can obtain topographic maps for $4 apiece from the:

U.S. Geologic Survey
Denver Federal Center
Box 25286
Denver, CO 80225
Phone: 800-435-7627

There is a $3.50 handling charge per order, which covers as many maps as you wish.

Sporting goods stores and travel book stores will often carry topographic maps from nearby areas. A California company called MAPLINK, in Santa Barbara, carries 60,000 topographic maps from around the world, and charges $6 per map. (MAPLINK, 30 S. La Patera Lane, Unit 5, Santa Barbara, CA 93117. Phone: 805-692-6777.)

Free Maps

Maps may be obtained free of charge in lobbies of motels and hotels and at airport information counters. One phone call to the California Division of Tourism (916-322-2881) will get you free maps. Ask for the free *California Visitor's Guide* which includes clear and attractive regional maps.

EXHIBITIONS AND ENTERTAINMEMENT

Free weekly newspapers available in public libraries and convenience stores publish a complete guide to the week's entertainment. The *L.A. Weekly, S.F. Weekly,* and *San Diego Reader* are the largest publications of this type but each city has its own. The menu of jazz, blues, rock 'n' roll, classical, Latin, folk and international music is extensive, to say the least. Also, theatre, art exhibitions, restaurants.

MAINSTREAM ATTRACTIONS AND ADVENTURE ACTIVITIES

The following attractions and activities are listed by city, with postal zip code following street address.

* Anaheim, **Disneyland Park**
  1313 Harbor Blvd 92803, 714-999-4565, Theme Park $25-99

* Bakersfield, **California Living Museum**
  P.O. Box 638 93306, 800-CALICO, Historic Theme Park $2-6

* Buena Park, **Knott's Berry Farm**
  8039 Beach Blvd. 90622, 714-220-5200, Theme Park, $15-30

* Buena Park, **Medieval Times**
  7662 Beach Blvd. 90622, 714-521-4740, Restaurant-Show, $22-95

* Gold Country (Coloma), white water rafting
  American Whitewater Expeditions (800-825-3205) and **CBOC Whitewater** (800-356-2262), $50-250.

* Mammoth Lakes, **Mammoth Mountain Ski Area**
  P.O. Box 24 93546, 800-832-7320, Ski Lifts, $22-45.

* Monterey, **Monterey Bay Aquarium**
  886 Cannery Row 93940, 408-648-4888, Aquarium, $6-14

* Palm Desert, **The Living Desert**
  47-900 Portola Avenue 92260, 619-346-5694, Zoo, Gardens.

* Palm Springs, **Palm Springs Aerial Tramway**
  One Tramway Rd. 92262, 213-931-6301.

- San Diego, **San Diego Wild Animal Park**
  15500 San Pasqual Valley Rd, 92027, 619-234-6541

- San Diego, **San Diego Zoo**
  Balboa Park 92103, 619-234-3153 (one of best in world) $6-15

- San Diego, **Sea World of California**
  1720 South Shores Rd. 92109, 619-226-3901, Theme Park, $22-30

- San Simeon, **Hearst Castle**
  750 Hearst Castle Rd. 93452, 800-444-4445, Historic Museum

- Universal City, **Universal Studios**
  100 Universal City Plaza 91608, 818-622-3801, Cinema Theme
  Park

- Valencia, **Six Flags Magic Mountain**
  26101 Magic Mountain Pkwy. 91355, 805-255-4129, Theme/
  Water Park

- Vallejo, **Marine World Africa USA**
  Marine World Pkwy. 94589, 707-644-4000, Wildlife Theme Park

- Yosemite, **Ahwahnee Whitewater**, whitewater rafting (800-
  359-9790), $60-450, and **Yosemite Trails Pack Station**, horse-
  back riding (209-683-7611), $20-50.

SETTING UP A BUSINESS

Entrepreneurs from other countries who wish to introduce a manufac-
tured good to the United States' market will discover that the process
is not as complicated as one would expect, so long as you keep your
production abroad and work through a U.S. distributor. Hiring a
California attorney is also highly recommended.

The distributor acts as the manufacturer's representative. The
manufacturers thus free themselves from billing and collection. Key
questions in the "Distribution Agreement" are: duration of the relationship; methods of ending the relationship; and fair compensation
on termination. Some distributors want exclusive representation.
Your lawyer will help you decide on this issue.

219

Corporate Tax

By selling through a distributor, you the manufacturer, enter the market without paying U.S. tax. The U.S. Model Tax Treaty, found in California libraries or U.S. Embassy commercial libraries, explains the tax exempt status. Even if you use your own employee, who does not spend more than 183 days in the U.S. during the calendar year, he will not be subject to U.S. taxes on the salary you pay him.

Trademark and Copyright

First step in entering the U.S. market: determine whether your product trademark is already being used by someone else in the country by checking with the Patent and Trademark Office.

Customs

Again, you as the manufacturer need not be involved in this process. The distributor (as owner of the goods) determines the classification, value and country of origin. You may oversee the customs value of your goods (Harmonized Tariff Schedule of the United States – HTSUS). If you are from a "Beneficiary Developing Country," the Generalized System of Preferences allows preferential treatment for your product. All goods you export to the U.S. must be marked "Made in (Country of Origin)."

Antitrust

Courts usually find exclusive distributorships as reasonable, but there is a question of antitrust laws against monopolies. If you decide on an exclusive distributor (or the distributor requires exclusivity), your lawyer should confirm that there is no anti-trust violation.

Immigration

If you or your employees need to travel to the U.S. to meet with distributors, you/they will qualify for a B-1 business visa. As you can see, the distributor and your assigned lawyer take care of much of the red tape. Your job is to create/find a marketable product, find a reputable and aggressive distributor, secure an attorney, and ship the product to the distributor.

California's multicultural population and developed consumer base makes it an ideal place for testing the U.S. market.

Chambers of Commerce and Visitors Centers (CCVCs) will provide you with free information on local business regulations. Here are a few selected small and large California CCVCs:

- Arcata 707/822-3619
- Imperial Beach 619/424-3151
- Los Angeles (Downtown) 213-728-7222
- San Francisco (The Mission) 415/391-2000
- Venice 310/827-2366
- Berkeley 800/847-4823.

Your research should be done before you travel to the U.S. The ideal source of information for (1) setting up a business; (2) addresses/fax numbers of distributors; and (3) addresses/faxes of California Chambers of Commerce, is the Commercial; Library at the United States Embassy in your country.

If you are "new," larger, more complacent distributors might not want to take you on until you can prove you'll be successful (a "Catch-22," – how can you prove you're successful until you have a distributor?) Find other people who have sold products to the U.S. and have them recommend their distributors. Distributors have product and regional specialities, and varying commissions; before approaching a distributor, find his specialty through reference books in the embassy Commercial Library.

A typical problem for a successful product is that the quantity cannot meet a growing U.S. demand. It is here that you the manufacturer may wish to license the manufacture of the same product to others. Licensing both technology/know-how and product trademark requires the participation of a lawyer. Even with licensees, you the manufacturer can still receive royalties from federal tax. If you make sure you are legally protected in these two areas, you may actually free yourself from production responsibilities and benefit exclusively from royalties.

The downside is that if licensees become sluggish, you may have to establish an office in California/U.S. to revive sales. In this case, U.S. internal corporate affairs are governed primarily by state laws, and your local California Chamber of Commerce will direct you to the correct regulations.

Expanding your operations becomes more complex at this point, as it concerns corporate taxes and immigration. The good news is that your CCVB can guide you, and that U.S. officialdom is quite easy to deal with. Regulations are clearly stipulated, and all you must do is abide by such regulations. Often, a simple phone call to any government commercial agency will put the required forms and regulations in the next day's mail.

CULTURAL QUIZ

CALIFORNIA: TRAGICOMEDY

California is a tragic country – like Palestine, like every Promised Land.

—Christopher Isherwood

Consumerism as an artform, apocalyptic riots, mass suicide by cult members, famous actor caught with prostitute, O.J. Simpson, illegal immigrants suffocate in smuggler's trailer, homeless panhandlers, mass murders, the inevitable earthquakes.

NEWS ITEM: Friday, February 28, 1997.

Armed with automatic weapons and body armor, two masked men robbed a North Hollywood Bank and then tried to blast their way to freedom, spraying bullets into houses and cars as the world witnessed it on live TV.

223

The Los Angeles Police Department found itself outgunned. Nearly 350 heavily armed police officers and FBI agents converged on the Bank of America branch near Laurel Plaza to do battle with the two robbers. One of the robbers was badly wounded and bled to death. The other pointed his weapon at his head, pulled the trigger, and ended his life.

How does one live in a place like this?

California's defense mechanism is its sense of humor. Ever since Groucho Marx, Californians mitigate tragedy with comedy.

ITEM: A new anthology of contemporary California literature is called *Absolute Disaster*.

ITEM: A graffito proclaims: "There's nothing like senseless violence to snap you out of a depression."

ITEM: Following the L.A. riots, the only thing remaining intact on a burnt-out section of Western Avenue: a Bennetton billboard depicting a burning automobile.

ITEM: From her job at a major California bank, the author's wife phoned a local branch to obtain some information. A woman responded: "Sorry, you'll have to call back. There's a bank robbery taking place right now."

Only in Venice would residents consider the whitewashing of their graffitied walls as vandalism. Only in San Francisco would bicyclists protest automobile degradation of the environment by clogging rush-hour streets.

How will you adjust to California's contradictions? Let's take a Culture Quiz.

SITUATION ONE

An irresistIble opportunity arises: to open a small business in an ethnic neighborhorhood (grocery store, photo shop, etc.). You are not of the same ethnic background as the majority of the residents. The key to success is:

A Offer the lowest prices in California.

B Use trusted family members as employees, thus reducing labor costs.

C Hire neighborhood residents and get involved in community activities.

D Use state-of-the-art decor to attract customers.

Comments

A seems obvious, but it's the easiest elimination. In the U.S.A., small operations cannot compete pricewise with large companies dealing in volume.

D may attract customers but people choose small businesses primarily for personal service.

C will establish a rapport so vital when someone of a different ethnic group does business in an ethnic neighborhood. To economize by using family help could make a positive difference financially (B), but as an outsider in the community, you will lose a whole lot more in crosscultural rapport than you'd gain in nickels and dimes.

Best answer: C.

SITUATION TWO

You are a newcomer and want to make friends and become a part of the local social life.

A Get a job.

B Strike up a conversation whenever possible.

C Join an organization or register for a continuing education class.

D Expect to be the focal point of curiosity seekers because you come from a different land.

Comments

Nothing is wrong with striking up a conversation (B) but friendships here usually come from common interests rather than shared community. Casual conversations with no structured context are frequent but rarely develop into friendships.

In much of California foreigners are an exciting part of the setting (D), but there are so many of them that you will not stand out, even with a *sari* or a *poncho*.

The workplace is a primary breeding ground for friendships (A). Visitors not in a position to find employment may do enriching volunteer work as a viable alternative.

Americans tend to be structured in nurturing friendships. For this reason, joining an organization or taking a continuing education course (C) creates the optimal scenario for close relationships based on common interests. Even short-term visitors will find an organization (church, environmental, hobby) with activities relating to their affinities.

Best answer: C. Also valid when possible: A.

SITUATION THREE

You are encountering homeless panhandlers and do not know how to deal with this type of phenomenon. Should you drop them some coins or will they spend your contribution on cheap wine?

A Do not give money. You are not going to alter the balance of the world with piecemeal donations, nor change the life of an individual.

B Tell the panhandler to get a job, thereby raising his/her consciousness.

C Participate in a volunteer group that helps the homeless.

D If there are more people asking for money than you can possibly help, decide on criteria that will isolate those to whom you can afford to give.

Comments

A short snippet of advice (B) to a person in desperate need is absurd.

If panhandling were based on pure opportunism, then giving would be senseless (A). But in most homeless panhandlers in California have a reason for their being out on the street: war veterans carry the scars of battle, the mentally ill are left without social protection after government cutbacks. Extended families and communities that look out for their weakest members in traditional cultures are a rarity in California.

It may seem arrogant to make a personal decision as to who deserves and who does not. But with so many homeless residents in California, you may be obligated to make such a choice (D).

Participating in a volunteer group (C) balances give and take. You give your time and you take back a chance to become a part of a new community and work with generous people whom you would never have had the chance to know otherwise.

Best answer: C. Alternative: D.

SITUATION FOUR

You are driving 67 miles per hour (65 m.p.h. speed limit) on a freeway with three lanes in each direction. You are in the right, slow lane. You are being tailgated. What do you do?

A Continue and perhaps speed up slightly only so as to enable yourself space to change to the middle lane and let the tailgaiter pass.

B Speed up. Adopt the custom of the guy behind you, even if it means driving 80 m.p.h.

C Teach him a lesson. Speed up without getting too close to the car in front of you and then press on your brakes, watching your rearview mirror and getting ready to speed up again should the tailgaiter be close to crashing into you. He will get the message, that tailgaiting is foolishly dangerous.

D Signal and pull over to the right shoulder.

Comments

On-the-road therapy is fruitless; C is dangerous and irresponsible. The speed limit is 65. Speeding up (B) is only advisable to provide adequate space to change lanes. Traffic often flows at 10 miles or more above the speed limit but you are in the "slow lane." If this is your comfortable speed, the driver behind you has the obligation to change lanes.

The best practice is (A): change lanes and get out of harm's way. No "principle" is enforced by confronting a sociopath on the freeway.

Pulling over to the right shoulder (D) is only an option in an emergency.

Best answer: A. Alternative: D, but only when option A doesn't exist.

SITUATION FIVE

You are invited to a dinner party. With so many different customs, from hippies to Hollywood, you wonder how to dress and what to bring.

A   When invited, you may ask the host if the event is formal or informal.

B   A bottle of wine or bouquet of flowers is always an appropriate gift.

C   Don't bring anything.

D   Ask the host if you can bring a dessert.

COMMENTS

A, B and D are all correct. California's cultural landscape is so varied that some degree of improvising (watching what others do) will be necessary. Even if the host says "It's not necessary to bring anything," a gift is indeed appropriate.

SITUATION SIX

On an extended visit to California, you are looking for an old-neighborhood, pedestrian-friendly, cafe-culture location as a base for your travels. Choose:

A   Any of a few enclaves in Southern California.

B   Most places in Los Angeles County.

C   The High Desert.

D   Most places in the Northern California Bay Area encompassing San Francisco and Berkeley.

Comments

Both B and C are automobile-dependent expanses lacking in cohesive old neighborhoods. But there are a few enclaves (A) within Southern California that would qualify (see text). D is the best answer, and A is a feasible alternative.

FURTHER READING

Abelmann, Nancy and Lie, John. *Blue Dreans: Korean Americans and the Los Angeles Riots.* Cambridge, Massachusetts: Harvard University Press, 1995.

"Agreement on Mono Lake," *Audobon* (Jan 95), 21-22.

Amselle, Jorge, "!Ingles, si," *The National Review* (Sep 30, 1996), 52-53.

Athen, Gary. *American Ways: a Guide for Foreigners in the United States.* Yarmouth, Maine: Intercultural Press, 1988.

Barlow, Dudley, "Melting Pot or Tossed Salad," *Education Digest* (Mar 1996), 34-36.

Burek, Dorothy M. and Connors, Martin. *Organized Obsessions: 1,001 Offbeat Associations, Fan Clubs, and Microsocieties You Can Join.* Detroit: Visible Ink Press, 1992.

"California: the Ruling Class," *The Economist* (Sep 17, 1994), 28.

Cramer, Mark. *FunkyTowns USA: the Best Alternative, Eclectic, Irreverent & Visionary Places.* Annapolis: TBS Publishing, 1995.

Davis, Margaret Leslie. *Rivers in the Desert: William Mulholland and the Inventing of Los Angeles*. New York: Harper Collins, 1993.

Eisen, Jonathan and Fine, David. *Unknown California*. New York: Macmillan Publishing, 1985. See Stegner, Wallace, "California Rising," 7-11; Dunne, John Gregory, "Eureka! A Celebration of California," 11-26; Lapham, Lewis H, "Lost Horizon," 27-34.

Fish, Peter, "Hostel Takeover," *Sunset* (Apr 1996), 30-34.

"Gang Warfare: Dadz in the Hood," *The Economist* (Nov 4, 1995), 33.

Goodman, Michael, "Coastal Nostra," *Los Angeles Magazine* (Jun 96), 72-77.

Greenberg, Peter S., "My Kind of Towns," *Avenues* (Jan-Feb 97), 30-31.

Harris, David, "The Last Stand," *Rolling Stone* (Feb 8, 1996), 38-43.

Harris, Richard. *Unique California: a Guide to the State's Quirks, Charisma, and Character*. Santa Fe: John Muir Publications, 1994.

Hart, John. *Storm Over Mono*. Berkeley: University of California Press, 1996.

Hornblower, Margot, "Heartbreak Motel," *Time* (May 29, 95), 58-60.

Huth, Tom, "Sunset to Sunrise," *Los Angeles Magazine* (Nov 95), 114- 119.

Lanier, Alison Raymond. *Living in the U.S.A*. New York: Charles Scribner's Sons: 1973.

Loomis, John B., "Public Trust Doctrine Produces Water for Mono Lake," *Journal of Soil and Water Conservation* (May 95), 270-271.

Lupica, Mike, "Nomo, Mr. Nice Guy," *Esquire* (Sep 95), 72-77.

McDonnell, Patrick J., "Immigrants Not Lured by Aid, Study Says," *Los Angeles Times* (Jan 29, 1997), A3, A14.

231

McKinney, John. *A Walk Along Land's End: Discovering California's Unknown Coast*. New York: HarperCollinsWest, 1995.

Merl, Jean, "Judges Weigh Pact to End Water War," *Los Angeles Times* (Jan 27, 1997), A3, A15.

Min, Pyong Gap. *Caught in the Middle: Korean Communities in New York and Los Angeles*. Berkeley: University of California Press, 1996.

Muir, John. Muir books show his great love for the outdoors. His advocacy generated establishment of Yosemite National Park. Discovered numerous glaciers. First to map the high sierra. After losing the battle to keep the Hetch Hetchy from becoming a reservoir for San Francisco, he died in 1914.

Poole, William, "Return to the Sinkyone," *Sierra* (Nov 96), 52-55.

"Quenching Corporate Thirst," *Amicus Journal* (Fall 96), 4-5.

Ravitch, Diane, "Children in Prison," *Forbes* (Jun 3, 1996), 94.

Rodriguez, Richard, "True West," *Harper's* (Sep 96), 37-46.

Rodriguez, Roberto, "The Politics of Language," *Hispanic* (Apr 1996), 53-58.

Rolfe, Lionel. *In Search of Literary L.A.* Los Angeles: California Classics Books, 1991.

Sanchez-Beswick, Marta, "Calles Project Helps Lost Teens," *Hispanic* (Nov 96), 8-9.

Schwartz, David B. *Who Cares? Rediscovering Community*. New York: Westview Press, 1997.

St. Antoine, Arthur, "On-ramp," *Los Angeles Magazine* (Feb 96), 36-38.

Stillman, Deanne, "The Great Wide Open," *Los Angeles Magazine* (Feb 96) 66-73.

Takaki, Ronald. *A Different Mirror: A History of Multicultural America*. New York: Little Brown & Co., 1993.

Wilbon, Michael, "A Celebrity Goes Free," *Washington Post*, Oct 4, 1995, F1.

Winoker, Jon. *The Portable Curmudgeon*. New York: New American Library, 1987.

Zinmeister, Karl, "Dangerous Suburbs," *The American Enterprise* (Nov-Dec 1996), 18 (from *The Car and the City* by Alan Thein Durning, 1996.)

Zinn, Howard. *A People's History of the United States*, revised edition. New York: HarperPerennial, 1995.

"Zoning Kills Community Life," *The American Enterprise (Nov-Dec 1996), 13-14.*

THE AUTHOR

Author of poetry, books of fiction and horse racing, and articles on history and literature, Mark Cramer's travel and culture writing began in Latin America and continued in France.

He made no attempt to write about his own country until having lived abroad on three continents. The culture shock of returning home gave him added dimensions for viewing his native land. His first book on U.S. culture was *Funkytowns USA: The best alternative, eclectic, irreverent and visionary places* (1994). *Funkytowns USA* has been highlighted in such weirdly diverse media as scholarly journals, supermarket tabloids, *Playboy*, CNN TV, and numerous feature newspaper articles. Obviously Cramer has not found a niche. His first book for Time Editions was *Culture Shock! Bolivia*, an appropriately unusual country.

Culture Shock! California could have been called "Culture Quake! California" according to Cramer. "With hundreds of interacting and conflicting cultures and customs, life in California measures at least 8.5 on the Richter scale."

Friends and relatives of Cramer and his wife Martha wonder when they'll ever settle down. "We believe in settling down," he responds. "The fact that our son Marcus knew three languages fluently by the age of 10 proves that wherever we go, we settle down."

INDEX